Why Don't Woodpeckers Get Headaches?

# WHY DON'T WOODPECKERS GET HEADACHES?

*And Other Answers to Bird Questions You Know You Want to Ask*

**Mike O'Connor**

*Edited by* **Olivia H. Miller**
*Illustrations by* **Michael Chesworth**

Beacon Press, Boston

**Beacon Press**
25 Beacon Street
Boston, Massachusetts 02108-2892
www.beacon.org

Beacon Press books
are published under the auspices of
the Unitarian Universalist Association of Congregations.

09 08 07 8 7 6 5 4 3 2 1

This book is printed on acid-free paper that meets the uncoated paper
ANSI/NISO specifications for permanence as revised in 1992.

Text design by Patricia Duque Campos

Library of Congress Cataloging-in-Publication Data

O'Connor, Mike
    Why don't woodpeckers get headaches? : and other answers to bird ques-
tions you know you want to ask / Mike O'Connor.
        p. cm.
    ISBN-13: 978-0-8070-8574-5 (pbk. : alk. paper)
    ISBN-10: 0-8070-8574-X (pbk. : alk. paper)  1. Birds—Miscellanea. I. Title.

QL676.5.O26 2007
598.7'2—dc22                                        2006031106

# CONTENTS

## 2.
## Bread and Water
## and Other Food Issues

## 3.
## Roadrunners, Cardinals, Ospreys . . .
## and More Birds You Should Know About

## 4.

## Stuff . . . and What to Do with It

## 5.

## I Like Birds, but . . .

## 6.

## Mystery Birds Identified and Explained

## 7.

## The Off-Season

## 8.
## Information Nobody Should Be Without

# INTRODUCTION

## How in the World Did This Happen?

No one would confuse me with the world's most prolific book reader. When I do read a book, I usually dive right into it. I have no patience for reading the Introduction, the Foreword, the Preamble, or any of that filler they put in before the real book begins. What's the point? The Foreword is like the opening credits of a movie. Everybody comes to see the stars of the film perform, not to read the name of the production designer. I'd bet that even the production designer's family members don't want to see it. They already know the person's name, and at ten bucks a ticket, they'd rather get on with the movie.

With that in mind I won't be upset if anyone doesn't bother reading this. Heck, I'll probably never read it again after I finish writing it. I think the only people who actually read Introductions are the author's family and friends, hoping to see if their names get mentioned. Well, those people can also stop reading now because I won't be dropping any names. Just like the production designer, you know who you are and nobody else cares.

Over the past few decades I have answered thousands of questions about birds both at the bird-watching store that I run on Cape Cod, Massachusetts, as well as in a weekly newspaper column. The questions are diverse: How can I attract birds? How can

I get rid of the "bad" birds? Why don't woodpeckers get headaches? Why are the birds dropping poop in my pool? Answering questions is easy; the hard part is keeping a straight face.

The one question that should be asked but never has is why a guy who barely passed English class is allowed to write a weekly newspaper column. And more importantly, why is that same guy allowed to write a book? Those are two good questions. The way I look at it, with so many books out there written *for* dummies, it's a natural progression to have a book written *by* one. Besides, if having brains were a determining factor for everything, we would never have anyone run for president.

After finishing college in the late seventies (here's the part where I explain how I got into this bird thing) with a degree in psychology (really), I took a job that required me to work nights. Working the late shift meant I was off in the daytime with not much to do. Boredom caused me to take long walks on the property next to my house, the spacious woods of the Cape Cod National Seashore. (You can probably see where this is going.) Like most psych majors, I didn't know a thing about birds, nor did I care about them. But slowly those daily walks somehow got me hooked on birding. And amazingly enough, I wasn't ashamed of it.

Becoming a birder is not a big deal; anyone with no life can do it. But then a more significant event happened. I left my night job. Now not only did I have no life, I had no job either. In order to keep myself in birdseed, I took a job delivering coal for a friend. (Yes, you read that right: I delivered coal. It was my Dickens period.) I was impressed with my friend's business and thought it would be cool to actually own a retail business. But what kind of retail shop could a psychology major open? What would I sell—couches? The only other thing I knew about was birding. What about a birding shop? Yeah. Why not? Camera stores had the binoculars, hardware stores had the feeders, grain mills had the birdseed, and bookshops had the field guides. Why not put them all under one roof? And most importantly, why not have someone working there who actually knew something about the products?

This doesn't seem like such a remarkable insight today, but in the early eighties it didn't exactly sound like a hot idea. A store just for geeky birders? Who would go there? Opening a shop called Nerd World would have been more promising. When I told people my idea of a shop for bird watchers, they would chuckle and say, "No really, what kind of shop are you going to open?"

Now, over twenty years later, thousands of birding shops have opened around the country, and some are even being franchised. In a fairly short period, bird watching has gone from being an activity just for weirdos to an actual business and a respectable business at that. Who'da thunk it?

In the spring of 2000, a customer came into my shop. As with most customers, I didn't know his name but his face was familiar and we chatted a bit. At some point he mentioned that the local weekly newspaper, *The Cape Codder*, was changing formats and looking for new features. He wondered if I might like to write a birding column. I can't remember exactly what I said, but I'm sure it was something about how us big-shot businesspeople are much too busy with our inventory control and dusting. But the more I thought about it, I liked the idea. I got so many questions each week, maybe if I put the answers in the newspaper, I would spend less time answering questions and have more time for dusting.

I agreed to write Ask the Bird Folks, and a few weeks into it, the guy stopped by to say how much he liked it. Other people seemed to like it, too. Soon, a few other regional papers started running the column. Several Ask the Bird Folks questions were included in a book entitled *The Best American Science and Nature Writing 2004*. I'm still not sure how that happened.

As the weekly column became more popular I found that I had to constantly make photocopies of back issues for people who had missed a column or two and, for some reason, wanted a complete set. There were also other requests from people who were too lazy to gather their own collection. They wanted all the columns put into book form. Finally, after spending way too much time with the photocopy machine, I decided that the book idea might have some merit. It might be good to put some of the most commonly asked questions under one cover so readers would have a handy reference and I could save some money on copier paper. The result is a book that offers answers to basic questions people have about backyard birding: everything from food, water, and shelter to bird habits and habitats, how to identify birds, what kind of equipment to buy, and how to choose a decent field guide.

As I was organizing material for this book, I thought about the customer who had suggested I write a weekly column. I wanted to tell him the news about his idea becoming a book, but I didn't know his name. I contacted the newspaper and they sent me his name, which sadly was attached to his obituary. The gentleman, I found out, was Dan Perkes. Before he was a guy buying birdseed from me, he was a writer for the Associated Press who spent time working in Russia and became the AP bureau chief in Japan. He later became an AP vice president, spending years working out of a corner office at Rockefeller Center. This unassuming customer was an important person to a lot of people. To me, he was just a nice guy who liked to feed birds and who would sometimes stop and chat. But I guess that's pretty important, too.

For the most part, the questions and answers in this book have been lifted from my weekly columns. A few changes have been made in an effort to correct mistakes (how was I supposed to know cowbirds don't give milk?), to disguise a few touchy question writers' identities (suddenly, everybody knows an attorney), or to stay more current (apparently Millard Fillmore jokes aren't as hip as they once were).

Over the years we have had lots of really good questions, as well as some questions that made me worry. In this book I've tried to select questions that the average backyard bird watcher might want to know the answers to. We start off with ways to entice specific species (like bluebirds and woodpeckers) to come to your yard. We then move to everyone's favorite topic of discussion, food. Only here we are talking about food, as well as water, that can be used for attracting birds.

Everybody seems to have a favorite bird or one that just catches their eye. The third section contains questions about roadrunners, penguins, turkeys, and other birds that many people want to know more about or at least that they should want to know more about. Like any hobby, bird watching has a fair amount of equipment that goes along with it. These items are important so that shopkeepers like myself can make money. I have added a section on selecting feeders and birdbaths, as well as a section on choosing basic binoculars and birding books.

It has always surprised me that so many people can take a joyful hobby like feeding birds and turn it into a source of stress. This next section is dedicated to those people. Here I discuss topics such as dealing with larger, more aggressive feeder birds, plus everybody's favorite topic, squirrels. I've also added a few questions about things that are actually problems for birds, like big glass windows. Then there are the mystery birds, the birds that look like twins, like the Downy and the Hairy Woodpecker. Or the birds that people want to know about even though they shouldn't, such as the Aflac duck. I told you some questions worried me.

The onset of winter brings a whole different set of problems that birds must face. The birds that remain in cold climates and endure winter head-on have a constant struggle to find food. But it is no picnic for the birds that must deal with the perils of migration either. Lots of people want to know about how birds handle the changing seasons. Finally, we get into an assortment of odd topics, ranging from the myth about throwing rice and what to do about baby birds that have fallen from their nests to how fast birds fly and why they stand on one leg. Some people are just plain nosy.

Before you plow into the book, there's one thing we've got to get straight. You'll notice that some names of birds are capitalized (Blue Jay, Black-capped Chickadee, Yellow Warbler), while others aren't (jay, chickadee, warbler). That's because birds need to feel important and like to have their complete common names capitalized. Besides that, without a capital it would be hard to tell the difference between the bird's name and a colorful description of the bird. There are many warblers that are yellow, but only one has the common name Yellow Warbler. You may also wonder why the names of birds such as cardinal and catbird aren't capitalized. Okay, I'll say it again. That's because they are not the full names of those birds. As much as some people hate to admit it, there is more than one species of cardinal and catbird in the world. In order to distinguish them from the others, we give each one a proper common name, with capitals, which in this case happens to be Northern Cardinal and Gray Catbird. Got it? Good.

The information in the answers comes from every source imaginable: lectures I've heard, books I've read, people I've spoken to, customer feedback, and stuff I've seen on TV or overheard at the bus stop. Basically, anyone who has written, spoken, seen, or thought about a bird has contributed to this book, and I appreciate it. If, after reading the book, you still have an unanswered bird question, you could always come visit us on Cape Cod. I'll be glad to answer your question in person, if you bring me a snack. Either that or keep your ears open the next time you are in a crowd waiting for a bus. Those people have never steered me wrong.

# 1.

## Bringing Birds to Your Yard

Although I've never done a survey, I would guess that most people who feed birds don't really know which birds come to their feeders . . . and they probably don't care. Seeing the constant activity of birds flying back and forth is rewarding enough for them. Then there are those who have turned backyard feeding into something resembling a contact sport. If you have hummingbirds coming to your feeder, they have to have hummingbirds coming to theirs; if you have nesting bluebirds, they aren't going to stop until they get bluebirds, too. I like these people. They somehow believe if they keep spending more and more on feeders and birdhouses, they will get better birds. That's not true, but who am I to crush their dreams and stop their spending? In reality, getting hummingbirds, bluebirds, orioles, and catbirds is fairly easy . . . if those birds are in your area. You don't need to spend lots of money. Just don't tell those other people that.

## Everybody Wants Bluebirds

*Dear Bird Folks:*
*I would like to know how I can attract bluebirds to my backyard.*
*Is it best to attract them by providing houses or are there certain*
*foods I should be using to attract them?*

*—Joanie,* BREWSTER, MA

Both, Joanie,

You should offer them food and a place to live. It's hard for bluebirds to pass up both room and board. While you're at it, offer them a beverage as well. Bluebirds seem to go out of their way to drink and splash it up in birdbaths. One last thing: Bluebirds like an open area to hunt for insects. They would love it if you took a chainsaw and cut down every tree in your yard. But you may want to start off with a house or two and see what happens.

Bluebirds seem to be the bird of the decade. Twenty years ago the only bird people wanted in their yards was the cardinal. In the eighties, the mighty Red Bird ruled. But as the cardinal population grew, the obsession with them waned, only to be replaced by hummingbirds. The quirky little hummers quickly became the bird of the nineties. With the new century comes a new trophy bird: the bluebird.

As much as 90 percent of the original bluebird population was eliminated during the last century. The blame seems to be on the usual suspects: pesticides, land use changes, uncontrolled cats, and our fixation on attracting cardinals. Another problem was the introduction of House Sparrows and starlings. Those two aggressive species quickly drove the timid bluebirds out of their nesting holes. Things looked bleak until hundreds of volunteers put out thousands of nest boxes across the country. With that, the recovery was on. Today, the bluebird population has increased to a level where most of us have a decent chance of attracting a pair or two.

The most important thing you can do for bluebirds is to put out proper nesting boxes. When I say "proper," I mean a plain, simple box with a one-and-a-half-inch entrance hole. Bluebirds don't need a box shaped like a lighthouse or a fat woman bending over. They like things as natural as possible. (It's not that a fat woman bending over isn't natural, it's just not natural for a birdhouse.) Remember, bluebirds like open spaces; thus, a nest box should be placed in the open, on a post or isolated tree.

When it comes to feeding bluebirds, don't go too crazy until you're sure bluebirds are in your neighborhood. As with most birds, the key to attracting them is living in the right habitat. People who live in a fairly open and natural area have a good chance of attracting bluebirds; those who live deep in the woods or, like me, in grossly overdeveloped areas are less likely to attract them.

Three things customers most often report bluebirds coming to are water, suet, and sunflower hearts (hulled sunflower). That is what I would recommend you start with, Joanie. They are the basic ingredients of backyard bird feeding. With those three things, you will also get plenty of other birds, so it won't be a waste if bluebirds don't show up. If the bluebirds do show up, you'll be ready for the next step.

The next step is to get those crazy mealworms you may have heard about. Yes, believe it or not, you can actually buy little worms to feed bluebirds. Mealworms are often found at pet shops, bait shops, birding shops, or in the live worm section of your neighborhood market. Simply put a handful of worms into a dish or a specially made mealworm feeder. Bluebirds love mealworms and can put on quite a show scooping them up, especially when they are feeding their babies. If the idea of live worms creeps you out, you can buy dried mealworms. And if dried worms creep you out, you can buy little suet nuggets that resemble mealworms. That's right, they even sell imitation mealworms, which reportedly taste just like chicken.

I'd start with a few birdhouses, Joanie. Providing them a place to raise a family is the most important thing we can do for bluebirds. Just remember to keep the nest boxes simple and leave the fat lady bending over for the side of the yard that faces your neighbor's house.

## Catbirds, the Birds
## Everyone Should Want

*Dear Bird Folks:*
*This summer I have just fallen in love with the catbirds in my*
*yard. Could you please tell me something about these wonderful*
*birds and what I could do to keep them around?*
—*Rachel,* ST. CLOUD, MN

I'm with you, Rachel,

Catbirds are wonderful birds. They are my third favorite bird,
just after chickadees and the eagle on the $100 bill. Even with
the awful word "cat" in their name, it is hard not to like these special birds.

There are a few species of catbirds in the world, but the one
in your backyard and all of North America is the Gray Catbird.
The catbird, like the mockingbird, is a mimic, incorporating into
its own calls other environmental sounds and calls of other birds.
But unlike the clear, repeated songs of a mockingbird, the catbird's song is a jumble of disjointed notes and squeaks.
Somewhere in that mixture of sounds, you will hear the trade-
mark "meow" call that gives the bird its accurate but ironic name.

Like many birds of summer, most catbirds spend the winter living the good life along our southern coast, with some reaching
Central America. However, unlike many of the skittish returning
songbirds that hide out at the tops of trees or take off the second
we spot them, catbirds seem to actually like people. (Evidently,
they haven't gotten the word about us yet.) Catbirds approach
humans seemingly interested in what we are doing, all the while
softly chatting with such sincerity that they appear surprised when
we don't answer back.

For those of you who don't know, catbirds are a sleek bird, not
much larger than an oriole but not nearly as colorful. The name,

Gray Catbird, does them perfect justice. Except for a black cap and a chestnut patch under the base of the tail, the catbird is gray all the way. The birds are so comfortable with the gray look that both the male and the female have chosen the same outfit, making them identical.

Catbirds aren't fond of deep woods but instead prefer broken forest edges and hedgerows. Since breaking up the forest is what we do best, catbirds are often found near humans. And as any fruit grower will tell you, catbirds love fruit. Years ago, I made the mistake of trying to grow and actually eat highbush blueberries. The catbirds couldn't have been happier. In a fit of selfishness I covered the blueberry bushes with netting. Well, my net worked great for all the birds except for this one catbird. No matter what I did or how I adjusted the net, that one bird always found a way into the bushes. Then, during one out-of-control attempt to keep this bird out of my blueberries for good, I humbly discovered the reason the catbird kept finding a way under my net. It was not trying to eat berries; Mrs. Catbird was trying to get to her babies, which were hidden in a nest in my blueberry bush. I immediately took down the evil net and sent it off to Vegas so the showgirls could make stockings with it.

Besides their lust for blueberries, catbirds will also eat grape jelly and oranges. Another way to attract them is with raisins. A dish of dried-up old raisins seems to be irresistible to catbirds. Water also appeals to them. It is important for bathing and to help wash down those dried-up old raisins.

Your catbirds should be around all summer, Rachel, then they'll head south for the winter. I'm glad you like these neat birds because I sure like them, too. I just wish they had a better name.

## Bring on the Woodpeckers

*Dear Bird Folks:*

*I really enjoy watching woodpeckers. Do you have any advice on how I can attract them to my yard?*

—*Erin,* PUTNAM, CT

Good for you, Erin,

I like woodpeckers, too. However, most of the time I have to listen to people whine about how woodpeckers are eating their homes. It's funny how a minor thing like a massive hole in the side of a house can upset some people.

In your part of the world, you have three common woodpeckers that readily come to feeders, with a fourth species becoming more common every year. The confusingly similar Downy Woodpecker and Hairy Woodpecker and the distinct Northern Flicker can be seen just about anywhere. The fourth species, the Red-bellied Woodpecker, is also distinct, but not because of its red belly, which is more of a rumor and not a very reliable field mark. The Red-bellied Woodpecker is a southern bird that has been moving northward in recent years, perhaps to avoid the endless stream of northerners who have been heading south.

All our woodpeckers come readily to beef suet. Raw suet can be bought rather cheaply at a meat market. But raw suet spoils easily, so only use it during cold weather or anytime you want to enjoy the wonderful aroma of rancid meat. A less smelly, but a bit more costly, approach is packaged rendered suet. It is usually found in small squares with birdseeds built in. The packaged suet comes in all kinds of flavors, from blueberry to orange to root beer (for the younger birds). The flavors seem to be more important to consumers than they are to the birds. I'm sure the birds have little interest in anything but plain, greasy fat.

You vegetarian freaks out there can use soy suet, as soon as it's invented. Until then, peanut butter is a good alternative. Also, peanut feeders are becoming more popular, especially with Red-bellied Woodpeckers. Red-bellies love to eat from wire mesh feeders filled with shelled peanuts.

Although woodpeckers live in tree cavities, they do not readily come to birdhouses. Woodpeckers are primary cavity nesters, which means they like to excavate their own nest sites rather than use a birdhouse. Other birds, such as wrens, bluebirds, and Tree Swallows, are secondary cavity nesters. They act like avian squatters and depend on woodpeckers to make their homes for them. Without woodpeckers, the secondary cavity nesters would be standing in line for affordable housing, just like the rest of us.

This leads us to a simple thing you can do to help woodpeckers: leave your trees alone. Too many people treat their yard as if it were Kensington Gardens. They cut, prune, and mess with every tree within their reach and that's of no benefit to wildlife. A dead or dying tree is both a food source and a place to live for many creatures, with woodpeckers being at the top of the list.

Many of our woodpeckers do use the boxes we put out, but only to roost in at night. When it comes to nesting, they seem to prefer chipping out a fresh hole. Flickers are the most likely of all our woodpeckers to nest in an appropriately designed birdhouse. I've read that if you fill a flicker box with wood shavings, the flickers are more inclined to use the box since they are fooled into thinking that they are indeed digging out their own nest. In addition, filling the box with wood shavings keeps out the starlings, who refuse to do any of their own excavating. It must be some kind of union thing.

As I said earlier, many people don't like woodpeckers and won't feed them because the birds have a habit of drilling into houses. But I wouldn't worry too much about that. Woodpeckers don't play favorites; they'll eat your house whether you feed them or not. In fact, most of the people who complain about woodpeckers don't have feeders out. That will teach them.

Feel free to feed and enjoy your woodpeckers, Erin. They are among our most interesting backyard birds. However, if you do use that soy suet, make sure you hang it real high or you could end up with a yard full of vegetarians.

## It's Not Just the High Rent

*Dear Bird Folks:*
*I would like to get birds to build their nests in my yard. I have several birdhouses and I also have tons of birds. But rarely do any of the birds use my birdhouses. What am I doing wrong?*
*—Roger,* LONG ISLAND, NY

Okay, Roger,

The first thing you need to do is lower the rent. Things are tough right now and there is a limit as to what any bird, even a bird from the Hamptons, can afford. If dropping the price doesn't work, try advertising free cable. You would at least be guaranteed that my kids would move in.

Although I don't know what your birdhouses look like, Roger, I've learned that it doesn't make much difference. Conventional wisdom tells us that birds like a simple nest box. A basic wooden box, unpainted and without the silly little perch below the hole, is what the know-it-alls like me recommend. But for some reason, birds rarely check with me before they choose a proper nest site. All too often I hear about birds using a birdhouse that someone picked up for a quarter at a yard sale. And the reason it was being sold is because birds never used it.

The basic boxes are very good and I still think they are by far the best. Yet, I've seen birds living in all kinds of silly-looking houses. The important thing is that your nest box, no matter what shape it is, has good ventilation, drainage holes, an easy way to clean it out, and, of course, cheap rent.

The point of all this, Roger, and there really is a point, is that you probably aren't doing anything wrong; nature is simply unpredictable. Nature doesn't always do things exactly the way we think it should. I guess that's what makes it so wonderful.

While we are on the subject of attracting nesting birds, it's important to keep in mind that only a small percentage of our nesting birds use birdhouses. Most birds build their own nest in trees or shrubs. Having an environmentally diverse yard is far more important than having birdhouses built to perfect specifications.

In addition to houses, another thing that some nesting birds need is mud. The other day, I got a call from some lady who was upset because birds were eating mud. I tried to convince her that mud was low-carb and she should try it, but she wouldn't go for it. Robins, phoebes, and swallows fly down to pick up beakfuls of mud for nest building. Although mud is usually not in short supply, there are some years when birds struggle to find it. Put out a tray of mud sometime and see what happens. If you don't get a ton of birds, you should at least get a call from your snooping neighbor.

There are a few odd things that will attract nesting birds. Tree Swallows love white feathers. If you know anyone who has domestic ducks, snag a bunch of their feathers and scatter them around your yard. If there are any Tree Swallows nearby, they'll quickly scoop them up.

The last odd thing, and this one is really odd, is dried snakeskin. For some freaky reason Great Crested Flycatchers love to add snakeskin to their nests. No one really knows why; they just do. Hang up a few dried snakeskins and the flycatchers will love you. If you are fresh out of snakeskin, try strips of waxed paper. The birds will take that also. As crazy as this all sounds, it actually works. And the best part is, hanging snakeskin in your yard will not only attract flycatchers, it will make your snooping neighbor forget all about that tray of mud.

## Giving Birdhouses Some Direction

*Dear Bird Folks:*
*Someone told me that for best results, birdhouse openings should face east. Is that for real, is it a fairy tale, or is it perhaps for feng shui?*

*—Rick,* BOSTON, MA

What, Rick?

Feng shui? Huh? Is he that little guy who used to be on the TV show *Fantasy Island?* I didn't know he liked birds.

We get this question about birdhouse placement a lot, but to my knowledge there has never been a study that consistently supports any one direction being better than another. The rule of thumb is to mount your nesting box so that the hole faces away from the prevailing winds and thus away from oncoming storms. But predicting which way the wind blows in Boston is like trying to guess how long the latest Red Sox manager will keep his job.

On the East Coast, we get storms from all directions. Raw spring rains seem to blow in off the water from the east, warm heavy rains come up the coast from the south, and in the summer we get lots of thunderstorms from the west. Then, of course, we get those wacky Nor'easters that come from two directions at once. Don't ask me to explain that.

I have nest boxes that face every direction of the compass and most have had birds nesting in them. My more successful boxes face west. But most of my boxes face west for no other reason than that is where I can see them better. One of the main reasons many of us put up a nest box is to watch the parents fly in and out to feed their young birds, so my advice is to place your birdhouse where you can best see the opening. Mount it so you can see it from your kitchen window, your back deck, or your fiftieth-floor penthouse overlooking Boston Common.

## You Don't Need a Ladder to Put Up a Birdhouse

*Dear Bird Folks:*
*Is there a specific height to mount a birdhouse? I've heard that eight feet is the best height.*
— *Kathleen*, SORRENTO, ME

Sorry, Kathleen,
You heard wrong. Eight feet is not the best height. Although birds will certainly use a nest box that is eight feet high, the best height to mount a birdhouse is the height that allows you to clean and maintain it. I see way too many boxes at the tops of trees that are neglected because people are too lazy to drag out a ladder, climb up, and clean them out.

I think the best height is "head height," and by that I mean your head height, Kathleen. That way you can easily maintain the box without having to balance on a ladder or barstool.

With the exception of a few specialty birds like martins, nest box height is not as critical as most people think. I've seen chickadees nesting a foot off the ground and swallows nesting sixteen feet high. But both species would be happy to nest in boxes five feet high. And that's where I suggest you mount your boxes. We'll let the ridiculously high boxes be put up by basketball players, giraffes, and that guy Rick, who lives in a penthouse overlooking Boston Common.

## Got to Keep a Clean House

*Dear Bird Folks:*
*I have a question about birdhouse etiquette. I bought my first wren house a few weeks ago and I am wondering if the house should be left up year round. Also, should the old nest be cleaned out?*

—*Nanci,* LITCHFIELD, CT

Cool name, Nanci,

Pretty fanci spelling. I like it. You are probably surprised to learn that you live in Litchfield, but since your note didn't include the name of your town in Connecticut, I took it upon myself to supply you with one. I chose Litchfield because I have an uppity aunt who lives there. If there ever was a town that worried about "birdhouse etiquette," it would be Litchfield, so that's what I'm going with.

I have to warn you in advance, Nanci, that this could be one of those answers where by the time you finish reading, you may not know any more than you do now. In fact, you may even be totally confused by the end. But if you are willing to take that chance, read on.

Yes, you can leave your birdhouse out year round. There is nothing wrong with that. However (you are going to be seeing that word a lot), since Connecticut winters can be pretty nasty, the box may not last long if you don't take it down in the fall. Avoiding snow and ice will add years to the life of your birdhouse. Personally, I'd rather people leave their boxes out all the time because the faster a box wears out, the better chance I have of selling them a new one.

I'm not the only one who wants you to leave your box out year round. Many birds huddle in old birdhouses to survive cold winter nights. However, you said that your box was for House Wrens. If your box was truly built for House Wrens, with the tiny one-inch opening, no other bird will be able to fit inside. Since House Wrens pretty much migrate out of Connecticut for the winter, you might as well take your house down and save the wear and tear. All the other birds are too fat to use it. However, if you are the type who won't remember to put it back out in the spring, then you should just leave it up. How's that for confusing clarification?

Should the old nests be cleaned out? Better take some aspirin before you read this answer, Nanci. Yes, you definitely should clean them out, maybe. Old nests often harbor nasty mites and parasites that can be harmful to the next batch of baby birds. However, the Migratory Bird Treaty Act of 1918 makes it illegal to touch, harm, or disturb any bird, egg, or nest. Even old nests are protected.

A few years ago, a customer gave me his deceased father's nest collection. (Business was slow that year and he must have thought we were a museum.) Like a bonehead, I put the nests on display and within days the feds came in to tell me that I had twenty-four hours to remove the display, and they weren't kidding. I was forced to quickly make a huge batch of bird's nest soup in order to dispose of the evidence.

Right now you are thinking, "Huh? Clean out the old nest even though it is against the law?" Yup, do it. And, by the way, how's your headache? The Migratory Bird Act does protect old nests, but that part of the act is like those anti-ticket-scalping laws.

Nobody really pays attention to it. The purpose of the law was to protect active nests from collectors or from jerks who just didn't like birds. So, it's okay. I've yet to hear about anyone who's done hard time for cleaning out an old nest from a birdhouse.

Now the fun really begins. Old nests often contain tiny parasites that may be harmful to baby birds. It seems like a no-brainer to recommend cleaning them out. A fresh, clean nest should be more appealing and better for the birds, or so you would think. But some studies suggest that the opposite is true. Old, buggy nests may actually be safer for the baby birds. Why? Because the old parasites may eat the new parasites, and the new parasites are the real problem. Whoa! Has your head exploded yet?

Most experts still lean toward keeping your boxes clean and actually I kind of do, too. However, you wouldn't be out of line or even qualify as lazy if you skipped cleaning your birdhouses once in a while. If, after all this, you still aren't sure what to do, check with the Litchfield Town Hall. I'm sure they have an ordinance about it.

## Purple Martin Houses
## Aren't for Everyone

*Dear Bird Folks:*

*I was shopping at Bowe's Depot-mart\* last week and saw that they had Purple Martin houses on sale. I was going to buy one but they seemed to be a lot of work to install, not to mention that I have never seen a Purple Martin in my life. If I invest in a martin house do you think that I would actually get martins?*

*—Sofia, upstate* NY

\*Note: Bowe's Depot-mart is not the name that Sofia used in her question. She actually wrote the real name of one of those cold, hideous, sprawling places that are about the size of the Pentagon. However, to prevent a misconstrued endorsement or perhaps a lawsuit, I decided to insert a pseudo-name. This way, no one will have any idea which store we are talking about.

A question for you, Sofia:

What are you doing shopping at Bowe's Depot-mart? Those people don't know anything about birds. If you were to ask one of their clerks in upstate New York about martins, he or she would probably think you were talking about Billy Martin, the successful but totally psycho baseball manager who was hired and fired by the Yankees five times. You may want to visit a specialty nature shop instead. They specialize in useful information about birds, whereas places like Bowe's specialize in massive asphalt parking lots.

Okay, now that I've finished telling you how to live your life, let me tell you a little bit about Purple Martins. Like Tree Swallows and bluebirds, Purple Martins are "secondary" cavity nesters. Unlike woodpeckers, which dig out their own cavities, secondary cavity nesters don't have the tools or the desire to do all that work. They simply move into an old cavity that no one else is using, replace the curtains, and they are good to go. The problem for martins is that they like to breed in colonies. A single cavity or two isn't good enough for them; they need a bunch.

Native Americans were the first to offer artificial nests to martins. They often used large gourds for carrying drinking water. When the empty gourds were hung up to dry out, the martins moved right in. Not wanting to drink from anything that birds had been nesting in, the Native Americans let the birds have the gourds and instead drank out of the plastic tumblers they bought at the last Tupperware party.

The Native Americans, as well as the subsequent pasty Europeans, learned to look forward to the arrival of martins. Martins are a welcome sign of spring, are totally enjoyable to watch, and eat lots of insects. Why not offer them some decent housing?

Should you put out a martin house, Sofia? Maybe. On my travels through upstate New York, I've seen lots of martin houses so it would be safe to assume that martins nest fairly close to your area. To verify that, contact a local bird club, Audubon Society, or birding store and ask for guidance. But I wouldn't bother asking at Bowe's.

Yes, martin houses are a bit of work. You don't simply run out and nail one to a tree during a *Price Is Right* commercial break. The boxes require proper planning and placement. Once you decide martins are in your area, you need to figure out if your yard is right for them. The good news is that martins really like people, goodness knows why, and they prefer to nest within a hundred feet of a house or building. Also, your yard should be fairly open, without trees too near the box.

Installation is where the fun really begins. Some of the multi-room martin houses require hours of assembly and the minimum fifteen-foot poles often need to be anchored in cement. But, hey, who doesn't enjoy hours of assembly and mixing bags of cement?

And that's just the beginning. The most successful boxes are monitored regularly, once a week or more. Monitoring typically involves checking for parasite infestation and removing any unhatched eggs or dead chicks. It's a lovely way to start the day. Then there is the problem of keeping out the starlings and the House Sparrows. Good luck with that.

I'm not trying to talk you out of putting up a martin house, Sofia. On the contrary, martin houses are critical to the bird's survival. It is believed that the Eastern subspecies of Purple Martins depends entirely on artificial nesting sites. If we took down all the boxes tomorrow, this subspecies might die out. The reason I made putting up a martin house sound like a lot of work is because it is a lot of work, and also because you asked.

But more importantly, since the species depends on us for its survival, we should do things right. Plus, if you do a lousy job setting up your martin house, all your neighbors will think you buy your nature products at Bowe's. Nobody wants that.

## Plant a Tree, Even If It's Dead

*Dear Bird Folks:*
*I'm feeling guilty about taking our Christmas tree to the dump after only two weeks. Is there something I can do with the tree that will benefit the birds?*

—*Judy,* BARRINGTON, IL

Me too, Judy,

I used to feel guilty about tossing out our Christmas tree each year. It seemed like such a waste, especially since we used very expensive artificial trees. Man, was my wife mad at me. After a few years, I finally caught on and stopped throwing away the tree but that's only after we switched to real trees. Then my wife was even madder at me. But the birds weren't; they liked keeping the old tree around. At last, no one was mad at me. Too bad they aren't better cooks.

I've never been to Barrington, Judy, but I've been to that part of Illinois and as I remember, it was pretty flat and open. An extra tree for shelter would be much appreciated by the birds that were trying to survive one of your northern Illinois winters.

I know many people, including myself, who put their used Christmas tree in the backyard for the birds. I usually set up the old tree near the feeder to help break the wind and to give the birds additional cover from hawks. It's easy to do. Simply stick the tree in the snow and walk away. If you don't have any snow that year, just cut a hole in a fruitcake and use that as a stand. No wind is strong enough to blow a fruitcake over.

I'm glad you are into recycling, Judy. Using your old tree to protect the birds during the long, cold winter is a great idea, especially for people like you who live in the frigid Chicago area. Just remember that when you set out the tree, take off all the old tinsel and in your case, remove those ornaments shaped like Mike Ditka. We want to help the birds, not scar them for life.

## Landscaping for the Birds

*Dear Bird Folks:*
*I just bought a new house and I would like to add some plants*
*and landscaping to my yard that will help attract birds. Do you*
*have any suggestions?*

—*Carl,* CHATHAM, MA

Congratulations, Carl,

Congratulations on your new house. Also, congratulations on wanting to create a better habitat for birds. But before we get into this, you should know one thing. I don't know anything about plants. You would think that a big sissy vegetarian like me would know everything about plants, but you would be wrong. That will teach you to stereotype.

Don't worry, though: not knowing about something has never stopped me from writing about it before. Although at some point, Carl, you will need to visit a garden shop or nursery to get some specific information to add to my forthcoming vague advice. If you have agoraphobia and tend to avoid shopping, a good book, which I use, is *American Wildlife & Plants,* published by Dover. This helpful fifty-year-old book is still in print and probably can be found at most libraries.

Birds have four basic needs: food, water, cover, and shelter. Wait, cover and shelter are the same thing. Change that to three basic needs. Most of what birds need comes from plants. I can't imagine a plant of any kind that doesn't benefit a bird in one way or another. When I say plants I'm including trees, shrubs, flowers, grasses, and weeds. A plant can be used for nest building, to roost in, and to provide berries or seeds for eating. Plants also attract insects that birds love.

When looking for plants in your area, think native. Seek out plants that are normally found around there or at least grow in a similar habitat. If you buy a plant that requires extra watering, fertilizer, and pesticides, you will do the birds and the environment more harm than good. Keep in mind who the plant is for. If one of your plants is being eaten by bugs, don't spray it; let the birds eat the bugs. The idea is to attract birds, not to have showy plants. Every year I talk to people who want to buy a birdhouse for the House Finches that are nesting in their hanging plant. They want the birds to leave the plant alone and move into the birdhouse. I say, "Hello? Get a clue. If they like your hanging plant, let them have it." A hanging plant is probably cheaper than a birdhouse, which the finches probably won't use anyway.

For years, most yards around Cape Cod were basic, low maintenance, and "naturally" landscaped. Pine needles protected the thin topsoil, and bayberry bushes and scrub oak served as borders along property lines. It wasn't that Cape Codders were lazy, but they had better things to do with their time than unnecessary yard work. Then, when no one was looking, it all changed. In came the lawns, fancy bushes, leaf blowers, fertilizers, and pesticides. Suddenly people stopped enjoying wildlife and started struggling with it.

Now I hear "The deer are eating my Queen Victoria rose bushes!" or "The skunks are digging up my perfect Scotts lawn, somebody help me!" No one ever complained about skunks digging up pine needles or deer eating scrub oak. Native is better. The idea is to support nature, not to fight it.

Diversity is also important. A greater variety of plants will support a greater variety of birds. Different plants will fruit or go to seed at different times of the year. Variety allows you to provide something for the birds in every season.

Finally, keep in mind that dead plants are just as important to birds as live ones. Don't be in a hurry to cut down every dead tree in your yard. Dead trees are a magnet for woodpeckers and birds that use woodpecker holes, including owls. Bugs like dead trees, too, and birds love bugs. The best thing about a dead, rotting tree is that it doesn't require any watering, fertilizer, or pesticides. The only thing you need to do is to take care not to park your new Porsche underneath one on a windy day.

# 2.

# Bread and Water and Other Food Issues

For years the stereotype of a bird watcher was a person with no life who crawled through swamps and had bad fashion sense. Well, as scary as it may be, those people are still out there, but in recent years many of the more normal people have become backyard bird watchers. By putting out a feeder or two, people have discovered that they can enjoy birds without being total freaks. Feeding birds brings them right to our yards, making it unnecessary to crawl through any swamps to see them. And the best part is that it's easy. Simply put out the right food and the birds will come and get it, no questions asked. The key is putting out the *right* food. There are choices to be made and sometimes what is sold as "birdseed" isn't the best choice. The worst offender is mixed birdseed. Mixed seed is the extended warranty of the bird-feeding world. It is overpriced, not worth much, and totally unnecessary. And for once, I'm not kidding.

## The Best Birdseed: Keep It Simple

*Dear Bird Folks:*
*I bought some seed last month at a local hardware store and most*
*of it is still lying on the ground underneath my feeder, uneaten.*
*The seed was on sale, but it looked fine. The bag contained sev-*
*eral varieties of seeds and it even had pictures of cute birds on the*
*label. This might sound like an obvious question to you, but are*
*there good and not-so-good types of birdseed? Was buying the seed*
*on sale at a hardware store a mistake?*

—*Peter,* SILVER SPRING, MD

Hardware store, Pete?

You buy your bird food at a hardware store? Where do you buy
your own food, Jiffy Lube? Maybe that's a little harsh, but you see
my point, don't you? The hardware guy knows everything about
nails, cement, and putty, so we can't expect him to know about
birdseed, too. That needs to be left to the birdseed professionals,
like us. I don't mean to suggest that you need a degree from
Johns Hopkins to understand birdseed. A degree from the
University of Maryland would probably be good enough.

The only thing you need to know about birdseed is never fill a
feeder with mixed seed and you'll be fine. There is no such thing
as a good feeder mixture. All mixes are wasteful and some are
plain awful. Low-end seed dealers "water down" their products
with everything from wheat to sorghum to paper chads found in
a warehouse in Florida.

Why is the traditional birdseed so bad? Not all mixes are evil;
they just aren't necessary. All birds have a particular seed they
prefer. Mixing in stuff they don't like isn't going to fool them. Just
because we can trick a dog into eating a heartworm pill by dipping it in peanut butter, that doesn't mean birds are as easily
fooled. At best, unwanted seeds are tossed onto the ground; at

worst, the seed clogs the feeder. No matter how many wonderful ingredients are in a mixture or how terrific the manufacturer claims it is, there will always be one favorite type of seed and all the others will be tossed.

Many years ago, my in-laws used to buy a half-gallon box of ice cream called "Neapolitan." Inside the container were three equal sections of chocolate, vanilla, and strawberry ice cream. On any given day there would be four or five of these half-gallon containers of Neapolitan in their freezer, each with the chocolate neatly scooped out. The strawberry and vanilla were always left untouched, but the chocolate was long gone. Mixing in bad food with good doesn't fool anybody, not even in-laws. They left the boring ice cream for the lowly company, me.

The best way to feed birds is with single ingredients. A feeder filled with their one favorite food is the least wasteful way to go. I know it seems boring, forcing birds to eat the same thing day in and day out, but food boredom is not an issue for birds. They are just glad to get it. And remember, we are not their only food source. Birds supplement their feeder diets with other food they find in the wild.

Now you are thinking, "Fine, we got the point already. Just tell us what food to put in our feeders." That all depends on which part of the country you live in. In the East, sunflower is the seed of choice with black-oil sunflower the most popular. Hulled sunflower, a.k.a. sunflower hearts, is also popular and leaves no empty shells on the ground. It is the perfect seed for all you neat freaks out there. The more traditional striped sunflower is okay, but the thick, heavy shells will leave a huge mess under your feeder.

If you live in an area that has lots of native sparrows, you might find a feeder filled with millet works better than sunflower seeds. Whatever works is fine but still, I would fill a feeder with only one ingredient to avoid the mess from less popular seeds being tossed onto the ground. If you want to feed ground birds like quail, doves, or sparrows, scattering small amounts of mixed seed is fine. Just try not to put out more than the birds can eat. If you have yellow piles of seed on the ground, I'd say you are over-doing it.

Fill your feeders with sunflower seed, Peter, or any other sin-gle seed that your birds are willing to eat. Once you find a good seed (probably sunflower), stick with it. There really isn't any other ingredient you can add to improve it, except maybe choco-late ice cream. But then you run the risk of having my in-laws eat-ing out of your feeder.

## Feeding Bread to Birds Is Sometimes Good, Sometimes Not So Good

*Dear Bird Folks:*
*When I was young, before feeding birds became popular, my grandmother would put out bread and other table scraps on a tray to feed the birds during the winter. Her birds seemed to love it. Yet, I don't see this done much anymore. Is bread safe or are we better off only using birdseed?*

—*Gretchen,* MANSFIELD, MA

Great, Gretchen, just great.

The slipping economy isn't bad enough, now we have you sug-gesting that people quit buying birdseed and start feeding birds table scraps. Swell. You can be the one to tell my ten-year-old son that twenty years from now, when he finally makes it through high school and at last can go off to college, there won't be any money to send him because people started feeding scraps to birds instead of buying birdseed. Thank you very much, Gretchen. Now he'll be living at home forever. I hope you're happy.

Actually, I'm glad to answer your question. I, too, have fond memories of my own grandmother putting out leftovers for birds. She had this big tray feeder on top of a pole in her yard. I would sit for hours watching the birds come from all directions on a snowy winter's day. However, I must warn you that this will be one of those answers that will contradict itself so often that even if you manage to read the whole answer, you are probably going to know less than before you started. You know, like what happens with most of the answers I write.

There is nothing wrong with putting a little bread out for the birds once in a while. It's a great way to use up old bread and to save a few bucks on birdseed. (Grrrrr!) The key phrase here is "once in a while." Many birds love white bread, but as our late pal Dr. Atkins would have told you, white bread isn't all that good for us or them. White bread is mostly empty calories. Just like my mother would always say when we went out for dinner, "If you fill up on bread, you won't eat your dinner." That was usually followed by "Get your elbows off the table, quit kicking your sister, and put that gum back under the chair where you found it." Elbows and gum aren't usually big issues for birds, but filling up on bad food can be.

Birds are totally capable of finding a balanced diet themselves. But when the weather is bad, the days are short, and foraging time is limited, a bellyful of bread might not give the birds the energy they need to make it through a frigid night. Birdseed, on the other hand, is full of the fat and protein that birds find in nature. So yes, many birds eat bread, but no, too much is not a good thing. However, a few broken-up slices once in a while are fine.

Better alternatives from the human pile of table scraps are doughnuts. A plain doughnut is actually better for birds than it is for us. All the extra fat that makes us look like, um, a bunch of fat doughnut eaters, is good for the birds. Remember, plain doughnuts are fine but sugared doughnuts should be avoided because they will rot the birds' teeth. Another good alternative is piecrust. Chunks of cooked eggs seem to be popular also. Although you would think that eating eggs would go against some kind of unwritten bird code.

The biggest problem with feeding birds bread, eggs, pie, etc. is spoilage. Even though birdseed can become dangerously moldy if not kept dry, seed will hold up much better outside than a plateful of scrambled eggs. None of the alternative foods does well during warm weather or when it rains. Your best time to try it is on a cold, dry winter's day.

It is important to remember that if you feed birds any leftover people food, you should only put out small amounts, once in a while. Any food more than a few days old should be cleaned up or soon your yard will look like the dumpster behind the bus station. And instead of cute birds you will end up feeding starlings, gulls, and, at high tide, barracuda.

## Feeding Peanut Butter to Birds Is Safe . . . If the Birds Don't Have Allergies

*Dear Bird Folks:*
*Is it okay to feed birds peanut butter? I've heard that birds have trouble swallowing peanut butter and could choke. I'm worried that I might be harming the birds. Is it safe to use?*
*—Marie, WATERBURY, CT*

Yes, Marie,
Peanut butter is safe to use. Every once in a while this question pops up and I'm not really sure where it comes from. I've never

found a dead bird with a PB&J sandwich clutched in its claws. And I have yet to hear of anyone who had to Heimlich a nuthatch. I did see a guy give mouth-to-beak resuscitation to a cardinal once, but that was at a party.

Remember, birds don't take the same size bites that an adult human would. They take little pecks that they can easily manage to swallow. Just like you probably take smaller bites than someone like Mike Tyson or Homer Simpson.

Feeding peanut butter is popular. I think every Boy or Girl Scout on the planet has had to smear a pinecone with peanut butter and then roll it around in birdseed to earn some kind of merit badge. Most feeder birds like peanut butter. And since birds have a poor sense of taste, it's up to you whether you want to use the expensive stuff they sell at the health food store or that five-gallon-for-a-nickel brown goo that you find at Willie's Warehouse World.

So use all the peanut butter you want, Marie. The birds will be fine if they eat it . . . although, they may sing with a lisp for the next few minutes.


## Oranges Attract Two Cool Birds

*Dear Bird Folks:*
*I put half an orange out, hoping to attract an oriole. It's been a few days, but no orioles so far. However, a catbird found the orange and seems to be enjoying it. I didn't know that catbirds liked oranges?*

*—Jay,* ROCKY HILL, CT

Now, Jay,
No one is ever going to confuse me with an English teacher. A

bodybuilder maybe, but never an English teacher. Still, I'm pretty sure that putting a question mark at the end of a statement doesn't automatically qualify it as a question. Your last sentence— "I didn't know that catbirds liked oranges?"—really isn't a question. It's more of a declaration or an admission. I even tried saying it in a questioning tone while raising my eyebrows, and I still couldn't make it sound like a question. Try it if you don't believe me and see for yourself. It's okay. I'll deal with it this time, but if you tried something like this on *Jeopardy* you'd be going home without any cash and perhaps without any lovely parting gifts.

Even with all this confusion I'm glad you wrote, Jay, because your question/statement reminds me of a question that we get all the time: "When is the best time to feed birds?" My answer is always the same: "Feed birds anytime you want, but May is the fun time." May is when many birds look their best and when unusual, hungry migrants may stop at our yards looking for a quick snack before they continue on to their breeding grounds. In May, my phone is lit up with calls about Indigo Buntings, Rose-breasted Grosbeaks, and Scarlet Tanagers that have stopped in peoples' yards, only to disappear after a few days. And May is when we see the return of hummingbirds, orioles, and catbirds, three of the most handsome and interesting birds you'll ever see at your feeders.

May is also when we can try new foods, other than sunflower seeds, to attract birds. Oranges are one of those foods. If you've never tried an orange, here's what to do. Search the back of your refrigerator, behind the outdated container of rhubarb yogurt you bought on sale, and find that one last orange from the case your Florida relatives sent you for Christmas. Cut that orange in half and nail it to a branch, tree trunk, or porch railing. With any luck, you'll be treated with a visit from a striking Baltimore

Oriole, or in your case, an oriole that was apparently wearing a catbird suit.

Jelly is another food to put out in May. Orioles, catbirds, and even tanagers will come to a cup of jelly. El cheapo grape jelly works fine, but feel free to use organic if you want to impress the neighbors. There has been some concern recently that jelly is actually too sweet for birds and that the high concentration of sugar found in jelly could possibly do them harm in the long run. It is thought that low-sugar jelly might be a better option. Remember, we are talking about low- or reduced-sugar jelly, not that artificial sweetener crap.

Then there are those delicious creepy, crawly mealworms, which you may remember me mentioning when I was talking about bluebirds. Mealworms are nothing more than harmless beetle larvae, but you can call them maggots if you like to freak people out. Most parent birds love to feed mealworms to their nestlings. The list of birds attracted to mealworms includes all that we have talked about already, plus bluebirds, wrens, and just about any bird that has babies nearby.

Caution: Don't be fooled into thinking that just because this food is different, you won't have squirrels trying to get to it. Even you know better than that.

May is also a good time to put out nesting materials. Birds love to use pet fur to line their nests. You can collect it from your pet and put it outside in a basket or net bag. Or you can do what I do. Simply open the window and let the birds fly in and pick the dog hair off the couch. The birds get a nice nest and I save on housekeeping bills.

Don't be disappointed if you get catbirds instead of orioles, Jay. But if you really want to put out something for the orioles that the catbirds won't care about, put out string. Orioles readily come for short pieces of string or yarn to build their nests. The key word here is "short," no more than six inches. If you use longer string the birds will be in danger of getting tangled, and you'll be in danger of some serious litigation.

## Nothing Beats a Hot Bath on a Cold Day

*Dear Bird Folks:*
*Recently you wrote about putting a heater in your birdbath so the water won't freeze in cold weather. I usually only put my birdbath out in the summer when it's hot and dry. Why would I want to put it out in the winter when it's cool?*

—*Ron,* TOPEKA, KS

Hey, Ron,

Do you only drink when it's hot and dry? What are you, a camel? Most creatures from around here like to drink on a regular basis (and I'm not just talking about the happy hour crowd).

Even though it can be dry in the summer, there are always ponds and lakes for the birds to visit. During cold winters, most available fresh water can freeze solid, leaving birds searching for water to drink. Sure, they can chip at ice or eat snow to obtain moisture, but consuming too much frozen stuff could make it tough for a bird to keep up its body temperature. That is why you rarely see any birds eating at Ben & Jerry's during the winter months.

The best reason to keep your birdbath open in the winter is that water will attract far more birds than even a bird feeder will. Birds that have no use for birdseed will come for a drink. Birds such as mockingbirds, waxwings, wintering warblers, or thrushes may come to your birdbath. A customer once brought us this great picture of a flock of bluebirds drinking at her birdbath on Christmas morning. And it was about a trillion degrees below zero that morning. Open water was tough for the bluebirds to find; just about everything had frozen up. Even the hot tub on the back of my limo had frozen over.

Don't forget, Ron, we do all of this for our own entertainment. If a summer birdbath works for you, then don't feel that you *have* to put one out in the winter, too. No one is going to talk about you. At least not until your back is turned.

## Backyard Birds
## Rediscover Bird Feeders

*Dear Bird Folks:*
*After being away from our home for long periods, the first thing we do is fill our bird feeders. Within hours, the birds are back feeding. The question is: How do the birds know that the feeders are filled? Why, after finding our feeders empty for so long, don't the birds put us on a blacklist and totally give up on us? I have asked this question to many so-called birders who can't answer it. I now pose this question to the only people who can.*

—*Schatze,* BRONXVILLE, NY

Oh my goodness, Schatze,

With all of the topflight birders and naturalists around, you are depending on us for your answer? Whoa, talk about pressure. However, you are right not to put any value on information provided by the "so-called birders." You can't trust what those guys say. Trying to learn something from so-called birders is like trying to get accurate information from Fox News. It's just not going to happen.

The first thing to keep in mind is that birds don't have a lot to do all day. They don't have tax forms to fill out, meetings to attend, or dogs to walk. When they aren't migrating or raising kids, the only thing on their to-do list is find something to eat, and that's it. Oh sure, there is the occasional pedicure or yoga class but mostly they are focused on finding food. Their two major sense organs, eyes and ears, are working overtime trying to locate their next meal. If they aren't able to visually locate food themselves, their ears are listening for the sounds other birds make when they find food.

Don't take this personally, Schatze, but your birds don't trust you and that has nothing to do with you being from New York. Birds learned long ago that no source of food is permanent. In nature things change and birds can't allow themselves to depend on anything. Your yard is simply one of the many places that birds check for food. If your feeders are empty, the birds move on. Sure, they may curse and take on a bit of an attitude but deep down they understand and won't hold a grudge. If your feeders are full, they will stop and eat for a bit, but then continue on, never allowing themselves to become dependent.

Banding studies have indicated that what we think of as "our birds" may actually be different moving flocks of birds that just look like the same regular birds. Years ago, I remember reading about a study in which finches were netted and banded. In the course of one winter, one yard and one feeder were visited by thousands of different finches. Even though only a few were seen on any given day, various flocks of similar-looking birds would show up every few days. After you fill your feeders for the first time in a while you may think that "your" birds are back, but it is quite possible that the birds on your feeder have never been in your yard before. You may be seeing a roving flock stopping for the first time.

Other birds, like our old pals the chickadees, don't fall into this random wandering category. The chickadees you see now are the same ones you saw last week and the week before that. Just like many of the less ambitious kids from your high school, most chickadees spend their entire life fairly close to where they were hatched. In the fall, chickadees form small flocks of six to ten birds, establish a twenty-acre wintering territory and rarely leave it. Thus, your chickadees are also your neighbor's chickadees. Even the creepy neighbor, the one nobody likes, could be feeding the same chickadees as you are.

When chickadees find food, they verbally pass on this information to others in their flock. It could be that these chickadees, the birds that know the 'hood best, are the ones that inadvertently alert other birds that you are back, your feeders are filled, and dinner is served.

Don't worry about being away, Schatze. The birds will always return and never put you on a blacklist. Not unless they see a Yankees bumper sticker on your car. Then you'll be on their S-list and you'll be washing your car over and over and over.

## Bird Feeding Rocks in May

*Dear Bird Folks:*
*Now that the weather is finally getting better, should I bring my bird feeders in for the summer?*

*—Tom,* MANKATO, MN

No, Tom,

Don't you dare bring in your feeders now. For us Northerners, May is the best month of the year when it comes to seeing different birds in your backyard. You never know what weird bird will make a surprise visit to your feeders.

Of course, it all depends on your exact location, but birds such as Rose-breasted Grosbeaks, Blue Grosbeaks, Indigo Buntings,

Scarlet Tanagers, Summer Tanagers, or any of the many brightly colored warblers could make a pit stop in your yard during spring migration. Some of the birds I just mentioned aren't necessarily attracted to your feeders, but the feeding behavior of resident birds may help attract them. Even my sterile yard, in ultra-suburbia, has had some really cool birds in May.

Whether you keep your feeders out year round or just during the colder months is really up to you. The birds are used to adjusting to our mood swings. They will be fine if you feed them every day of the year or if you only put your feeders out for one afternoon during Lent.

For entertainment's sake, Tom, I'd keep those feeders out for at least a few more weeks. May is the month we have all been waiting for. You never know when you might get some strange visitors. And when I say "strange visitors," I'm still talking about birds and not your wife's cousins from Duluth. They usually don't show up until August.

## Rotten, Moldy Seed Isn't as Good as It Sounds

*Dear Bird Folks:*
*My neighbor is always raking up the empty shells from underneath her bird feeders. She says it's healthier for the ground-feeding birds and it prevents the seeds from sprouting. I told her she is wasting her time. The seeds would compost themselves and the uneaten seeds probably won't sprout anyway. Am I right?*
— *Ann G.,* WELLFLEET, MA

Gee, Ann,

I know you are from Wellfleet, but even you can't enjoy eating out of a compost pile. Even though wet, rotting, moldy seed does sound appealing, it really isn't the best for the birds. I've read that breathing mold can cause respiratory problems for birds but more importantly, the seeds that are on the ground are mixing in with the droppings from the birds on the feeder above. (This is sounding yummier all the time.) Feeder birds can pass illnesses on to ground-feeding birds through their droppings. It becomes even more important to clean up under your feeders during wet, cold weather when birds are stressed and more susceptible to disease.

As far as the seed sprouting, that all depends on the kind of seed you use. If you use sunflower seed, then yes, a few seeds will sprout, but the worst thing that could happen is that you get your very own sunflower growing in your yard. But if you use hulled sunflower (sunflower seeds without shells) you won't get any mess at all. However, if you use a mixed seed, especially one of those one-hundred-pounds-for-a-nickel bags of junk that they sell at Cousin Tony, the Discount Dude's Barn of Bargains, you could have tons of things growing. The cheaper the mix, the more filler seeds are added, much of which the birds avoid eating, and thus, the more left to sprout.

And if you don't rake it up once in a while, you could have all kinds of mystery plants growing in your yard. Some of these might attract flocks of birds, while some of the weirder-looking plants may attract flocks of partygoers, who have a different use for the plants. You just never know what kinds of seeds are in those mixes. And if you think squirrels are tough to baffle, just try keeping those party dudes off your feeder.

So yes, Ann, you really should rake under your feeders and avoid cheap mixes. Sorry I couldn't take your side but for at least this one time, your neighbor was right. But don't worry; it probably won't happen again.

## Go Nuts with Peanut Feeders

*Dear Bird Folks:*
*I was thinking about offering peanuts to my birds but nuts are a*
*little pricey. Before I invest in buying expensive peanuts, I would*
*like to know if you think they are a good idea.*
— *Mitch, central* MA

First, Mitch,

I have a question for you. Are you from Worcester? Because only someone from Worcester would need financial advice before buying a bag of peanuts. I grew up around Worcester and we were so tight that even people from Scotland made fun of us. I've sold peanuts for years. Whenever customers buy a bag, I give them a look like they are drunken sailors throwing away their money. To me, there is no better or more popular food than sunflower seed. And most importantly, it's cheap. Why spend more money on nuts?

A peanut feeder is nothing more than a tube of fine wire mesh that holds peanuts like a suet basket holds suet. I have been blindly selling them for years, assuming that they work fine but have been too cheap to buy one myself. One day a customer pointed out that the holes in the feeder were much smaller than the peanuts. It would be impossible for a peanut to fit through the tiny holes. When the customer asked me how the birds got to the food, the only thing I could say was (in a dumb guy's voice), "Dunno." At that point, I knew it was time for me to turn my back on my thrifty past and try a peanut feeder.

I brought my new peanut feeder home and hung it up with all my other feeders, but the birds didn't seem interested. Days went by and the birds avoided it like a baked apple on a dessert cart. Finally, after about a week, a chickadee landed on it and tried to eat a peanut but couldn't get one out and flew away. The next day the same thing happened. I thought, "Oh man, that customer was right. These feeders don't work." I broke into a cold sweat thinking that it was only a matter of time before I would be dragged in front of the Federal Trade Commission. I could see myself doing five to ten for selling bad bird feeders.

To end the suspense and speed up this story, I should tell you that the birds finally did figure out the new feeder. It turned out that the birds don't pull out the whole peanut, like they do with sunflower seeds; they peck out little pieces like they do on a suet feeder. In fact, the peanut feeder is now one of the most popular feeders in my yard. All the birds love it, including chickadees, titmice, finches, jays, and woodpeckers. Since they are only taking little pieces, the feeder stays full longer and thus actually costs less to use than a sunflower feeder. My Worcester friends will be thrilled to hear that.

There are a few things to keep in mind if you buy a peanut feeder. The wire mesh feeders offer no protection from the weather. To prevent spoilage, you must keep your nuts fresh. Really. Use raw, hulled peanuts only; don't buy roasted peanuts, salted peanuts, or peanut brittle. Also, don't be confused and buy peanut hearts. Peanut hearts are nasty little nibs that are a favorite of starlings and not a whole bunch else. Since nuts don't melt like suet can, peanut feeders are a great summertime alternative for woodpeckers. Plus, the small holes in the wire mesh will keep the squirrels from eating too much, even though they sure like to try.

Go for a peanut feeder, Mitch. It is totally worth the investment. If you decide to buy one, give me a call. I know a place in Worcester that not only sells peanut feeders, they still give Green Stamps.

## Holiday Treats Make Edible Decorations

*Dear Bird Folks:*
*Instead of Christmas lights, I would like to decorate the spruce tree in our yard with some treats for the birds. We used to string popcorn, cranberries, and peanuts in the shell. Are those things good for the birds and do you have any other ideas?*
— *Marcia,* CRANSTON, RI

Great idea, Marcia,
Stringing treats for the birds is a fun family activity and

Christmas is the only time of year when you can get away with that kind of peculiar pastime. Any other time of the year you might get beaten up if you suggested spending a Saturday night running thread through hunks of food to be hung out in the yard. But in December, we all have that "Santa Claus is watching you" paranoia in the back of our minds and we don't dare say no to even the most ridiculous activities.

Of the three things you mentioned, peanuts are the big winner. Blue Jays love peanuts and the squirrels are happy to take a few, too. Before you have a fit and scream, "I'd rather eat glass than give $1.19-a-pound peanuts to a rotten squirrel," think about who is watching you. So, you'd better not shout or even pout. Popcorn is fine. Jays like it and crows do, too.

Cranberries are the losers here. Most birds, like most people, have little interest in uncooked, unsweetened cranberries. The bog people are hurting this year so I don't want to talk you out of using cranberries. Use tons of them. Just know that you should use them only for color and to stain your fingers red while you thread them on the string.

Better choices for fruit are dried apples and raisins. Robins and even bluebirds will eat them when the natural food supply is low. Pieces of doughnuts are another good item to string. You could attract chickadees, nuthatches, and maybe even a cop or two. I've heard of people stringing things like Cheerios and other kinds of cereal with a built-in hole. I guess that's okay although I'm not sure what you would attract, a starling or a toddler. But you shouldn't use sugar-coated cereal. Everyone knows that birds' teeth are extremely prone to cavities. Fruit Loops, however, would be fine to use if you have Toucans in your neighborhood.

Go ahead, Marcia, adorn your tree with whatever you want and be creative. Don't worry too much about what you use; the birds will only eat what they want and leave the rest. At our house we used to each make our own string of food for the birds. We would try to outdo each other and come up with the fanciest string of treats. Then we would bundle up, go out, and decorate a small pine tree. Some years it would be snowing; other years we'd have the full moon to light our way. We would be out in the cold night air decorating that tree for hours . . . or until the guy who owned the tree came home and chased us out of his yard.

## The Ethics of Backyard Bird Feeding

*Dear Bird Folks:*
*My ten-year-old daughter asked me about feeding wild animals. Her concern is that we are constantly being reminded not to by signs that read: "Don't feed the bears," "Don't feed the ducks," and in some places, "Don't feed the gulls." If all that is wrong, why are so many people feeding birds? Isn't feeding birds just as wrong?*

—*Peter,* ORLEANS, MA

Swell, Peter,

As if business this time of year isn't tough enough, now I have a ten-year-old trying to put some kind of ethical twist on things. This I don't need. Doesn't she have a video game to play or a younger brother to tease? What about a pony? Can't you get the kid a pony so she can focus on cleaning stables and not on the moral ramifications of bird feeding?

Actually, Peter, I'm surprised that I don't hear this question more often. It is odd that it's okay to feed backyard birds and not okay to feed many other forms of wildlife. Why? Well, first of all, there is the obvious danger in feeding some creatures. The number of people who have been eaten by bears is nearly three times greater than the number of people who have been eaten by chickadees. Except for the occasional, accidental hummingbird beak stuck in the eye or the woodpecker attack on peg-legged pirates, backyard birds are mostly harmless.

Everything that we humans do impacts wildlife at some level, either good or bad, usually bad. Feeding bears has caused them to lose their fear of people, which has led to unfortunate confrontations. In addition, if the crap we eat isn't all that good for us, it is probably detrimental to the long-term health of bears, too.

Many towns have posted areas asking people not to feed ducks. Feeding ducks on a small scale is fairly harmless, but when too much food is poured into too small an area, lots of problems can arise. A body of water can naturally support a certain number of waterfowl. When the available food is artificially increased, the duck population also increases. The extra birds can strip the area of all natural food, and their droppings can lead to a serious pollution problem.

I doubt if feeding gulls the occasional French fry has led to too many major environmental problems. The complaints about gulls mostly come from the snooty boating crowd upset with the gull's habit of contributing to the poop deck. It is the tons of wasted food from our open dumps and landfills that has increased the gull population, but that's another subject for another day.

Backyard bird feeding is also not without problems. I'm sure many birds die from diseases spread through improperly maintained feeders. Many other birds are attracted to our yards only to die from collisions with our windows. Then there are the millions of birds killed by our uncontrolled pets. Our yards are not always as safe as we think they are and birds suffer for it.

It's not all bad news, however. There is little doubt that feeders have expanded the range of many birds. Forty years ago, cardinals and titmice were rarely seen in the North. Without feeders to eat from in the winter, the only red creature brightening up the backyards in Maine would be an escaped lobster or two.

There is no getting around it; everything we do impacts every level of our ecosystem. Right now, the jury is still out as to the long-term benefits or problems caused by our backyard feeding. At this point, the good seems to outweigh the bad. It may be many years before the answer to this question becomes clear.

What is clear is that humans are the real beneficiaries of feeding birds. (I'm talking about real humans and not money-grubbing birdseed merchants like me.) For many people, birds are the only company they have on a cold winter's day. For others, backyard birds are their only or last connection to nature.

Your ten-year-old is right to question any and all of our dealings with the environment. I wish more people would do that. As of this moment, backyard bird feeding, although not perfect, isn't the moral equivalent of setting up oil rigs in the Alaskan wilderness. Maybe if we continue to be conscientious with our feeding practices, we will never need to post a "no bird feeding" sign in anyone's backyard. Then I won't have to quit the birdseed business and return to my old job, rounding up runaway lobsters in Maine.

# 3.

# Roadrunners, Cardinals, Ospreys . . . and More Birds You Should Know About

Birds are all around us. Our trees and skies are filled with hundreds of different species. Yet people often don't inquire about the birds that visit their own yards. The birds they want to know about are those they see on TV, in the news, or in cartoons. That's just fine with me because there is nothing I like better than having to watch cartoons for the sake of research. In the past few years, the hot-topic birds have been penguins, flamingos, and, of course, the born-again Ivory-billed Woodpecker. Besides those birds, coastal people want to know about ducks, desert dwellers like their roadrunners, and the glass-is-half-empty crowd consistently ask about extinct birds. Fortunately, there are enough types of birds to satisfy all interests. And if you don't have any particular interests, don't worry; I have included a question about cardinals just for you.

## Robins Are Not Boring

*Dear Bird Folks:*
*It seems like you guys always write about birds I never see in my yard. I have a rather small yard and the most exotic birds I ever get to see are robins. Will you ever be writing about robins or are they just too boring to write about?*

—*Sharon,* NASHUA, NH

Come on, Sharon,

I write about robins all the time. Although I admit most questions about robins are submitted in January, when every time somebody sees one, the "robins are back, spring is here" hysteria sweeps the North. By spring, the robin talk quiets down until the following January, when visits from wintering robins kick off another round of hysteria. All of this is fine with me, since I just reprint the same advice that I gave the January before. Ah, short-term memory loss . . . My two favorite types of readers are those with short-term memory loss, and some other kind that I can't think of right now.

The robin is one of the most common birds on the continent. It is properly referred to as the *American* Robin, not because it is an overly patriotic bird but because it was misnamed by a group of early settlers. The British, still seasick from crossing the Atlantic and high on tea, named one of the first birds they saw "robin." They thought our robin looked much like the English (European) Robin, which, of course, is stupid. Elvis and I look more alike than those two birds do. The American Robin is a ten-inch-long robust bird, while the little weenie English Robin is barely over five inches long and is rumored to be petrified of worms.

The American Robin can be found just about everywhere in North America. It ranges from the hot, steamy tropics of Mexico to the frozen world above the Arctic Circle. Tremendously adaptable, robins thrive in remote areas, hundreds of miles from the nearest human, or in the smallest inner-city backyard. Yet, whether they are deep in the lonely woods or in chaotic city parks, robins bring their cheery song wherever they go. And singing is what they do best. Any insomniac will tell you that the robin is the first bird to greet the new day. Long before the sun gets up in the morning, the robin, in the pitch dark, sings loud and clear from its favorite perch.

When we think of robins, we think of worms. Yet only about 10 to 20 percent of a robin's diet is made up of earthworms; the bulk of its diet is insects and fruit. The stereotypical image of a robin hunting is one of the bird hopping across an expanse of lawn and twisting its head side to side, "listening" for worms just below the surface. However, contrary to the old belief, robins do not hunt by listening but by actually looking for a worm exposing itself.

Cocking its head merely allows the bird to gain a better view of the area.

Robins have undoubtedly benefited from humans. They thrive on the fruit and ornamental bushes we plant. They also nest in the trees we have added to what was once the Great Plains. Yet, millions have fallen victim to uncontrolled pets or have suffered because of our love of the perfect lawn. No matter how innocent it seems, overuse of some lawn care products has been rough on robins, other birds, and perhaps even on us.

I think just about every child's first baby bird experience has been with young robins in the nest. Their nest is a fairly bulky woven bowl of mud and dried grasses. And, in what can only be described as one of the biggest coincidences in all of nature, the eggs they lay are all colored "robin's egg blue."

Robins are feisty when it comes to defending their territories. Some robins are so aggressive they will attack their own reflections on nearby windows. Attacking their reflections rarely harms the bird, but it does lead to messy windows and an endless stream of complaints to me . . . like it's my fault.

No, Sharon, robins are far from boring. Their song and their color brighten our yards every season of the year. That last line, "every season of the year," is important to remember. That will save lots of hysteria come January. Save that hysteria for something else, like madly racing to the grocery store every time they predict a bit of snow.

## Blue Jays Are Smart and Handsome . . . and No One Likes Them

*Dear Bird Folks:*
*Blue Jays are one of my favorite birds, yet many of my neighbors*
*complain about them. They say that they are nothing but mean*
*bullies. Could you please write something nice about them so I*
*don't feel guilty about liking them?*

—*Diana,* LONG ISLAND, NY

Sure, Di,

I'll write something nice about Blue Jays. I don't have trouble
writing nice things about any bird. It's your neighbors I'd worry
about. Talk about mean bullies. That's a pretty rough crowd out
there on Long Island. You don't want to get near any of them
before they've had their morning latte.

Blue Jays are clearly one of the most fascinating and handsome of all our native birds. There are few birds in North America
that can compare with their striking beauty. Yet other birds,
including the dumpy little Eastern Bluebird, seem to receive most
of the love while the Blue Jay draws the wrath. Apparently some
birds have better PR agents than others.

When Blue Jays land on a feeder, the smaller birds scatter but
that's more the result of the little birds being wimpy, not because
the jays are bullies. Have you ever seen a jay beat up another feeder bird or shake it down for its lunch money? No. The jays just
land and eat, ignoring the other birds. I think the little birds are
more startled than afraid. Most of the time the other birds quickly return to the feeding area, showing little fear of being attacked
or getting a wedgie from the big, bad jay.

The next complaint is that jays are pigs. They eat all the food
and don't leave any for the "good" birds. To me, any bird that eats
a lot of birdseed is a good bird. Of course, a large bird will eat

more than a smaller bird but that doesn't make it evil. And jays probably don't eat as much as we think they do. Jays have the ability to store seeds in a throat pouch, much like a chipmunk does with its face. The jay only looks like it is scarfing down tons of seeds, when actually it is collecting seeds to eat more slowly later. They also hide seeds in a "stash." (I think we all remember what a stash is.) Jays hide food for later use, which benefits other creatures that often find the stash and "borrow" seeds from it.

The biggest complaint about Blue Jays is that they eat other birds' eggs, or worse, they eat other birds' babies. In fact, I heard of one lady who was so upset when she saw a jay eating another bird that she nearly dropped her bucket of Kentucky Fried Chicken. While it is true that jays will occasionally rob from another bird's nest, it doesn't happen often. I'll admit that it's tough to watch a jay carry off a baby oriole but the jay isn't doing it to be mean or hateful; it is providing food for its own nestlings.

In fact, for the most part, jays are vegetarians. Researchers who examined the contents of hundreds of jays' stomachs found that only 25 percent contained insects and other animal matter. The other 75 percent contained nuts, acorns, seeds from your neighbor's feeders, and, of course, vegetarian-approved tofu.

There are several reasons why we should like Blue Jays. First, they are really beautiful birds. I know that sounds shallow but that's the kind of guy I am. Travelers from England often are thrilled to see their first Blue Jay, although I'm not sure if they are truly impressed with the jay's good looks or if it is just the first bird they've ever seen that wasn't shrouded in fog.

Jays also should be given credit for saving the lives of many birds. Your neighbors probably complain about this, too, but the jay's raucous call, "jaay, jaay," warns others when a predator, such as a hawk or the dreaded house cat, is around.

It should also be pointed out that Blue Jays are excellent parents. The male helps the female build the nest, he feeds her while she is sitting on the eggs, and he helps her feed the young birds after they have hatched. Blue Jays also stay together throughout the fall in a family group. They don't split up until spring, when the breeding season makes them all crazy.

One last thing you should know about jays is that they molt in late summer. Some birds molt so slowly that you can hardly notice, but sometimes jays will molt so rapidly that they lose their crest and become completely bald. If you see a bald Blue Jay, Diana, relax. Occasional baldness is normal and the feathers will grow back. There is no reason to panic or to call me about it. Also, don't waste your time mixing Rogaine in your birdseed to help stop the baldness. It doesn't work. Believe me, I've tried.

## Cardinals Mate for Life, Which for Them Isn't All That Long

*Dear Bird Folks:*
*What is the average life expectancy of a cardinal? Do they mate*
*for life? If one dies, does the surviving one take another mate?*
*—Dorothy, u.s.a.*

Whoa, Dorothy!

You sure are asking for a lot of information. What do you think this is, Twenty Questions? You people from "U.S.A." sure are demanding. Below is probably more information than you really wanted to know about cardinals. So, read this carefully because somewhere in this long, rambling reply you are bound to find the answers to your lengthy list of questions.

Believe it or not, the Northern Cardinal, despite its name, really isn't a "northern" bird and is a fairly new bird to many parts of the North. The first pair didn't nest in Massachusetts until

1958 and baby cardinals didn't hatch out in Maine until 1969. Apparently, cardinals figured that if people were brave enough to walk on the moon, they could handle a few weeks in Bangor. The cardinal is really a bird of the mid-Atlantic and southeastern states. For years Southerners referred to the cardinal simply as "the red bird." However, McCarthyism and the Red Scare, plus a class action suit by a group of Scarlet Tanagers, put an end to that. In recent years, the cardinal has been expanding its range north. I'm sure bird feeders have contributed to this expansion, but our suburban yards, with their shrubs and bushes, have probably helped the cardinals the most.

Back in the eighteen hundreds, cardinals were trapped by the thousands and shipped overseas to be sold in cages as pets. Fortunately, that practice was outlawed and our cardinals were saved. Now, we trap birds from other countries and keep their birds in cages here. And everybody seems okay with that. Everybody except the birds, of course.

One of the reasons we like cardinals so much is that it's easy to tell the sexes apart. When we see a male cardinal feeding a sunflower seed to a female, we think, "Oh, that is so sweet." But we don't feel that warmth when another bird, like a Blue Jay, does the same thing because male and female jays look alike. We don't know if it's a male feeding a female or a female feeding a male or whether it's a civil union or what's going on.

An unusual thing about cardinals is that both sexes sing and both sound basically the same. In most other bird species, the male will pick an exposed perch and sing to announce its territory. The females are happy to let the big-mouthed males be out there making noise so they can enjoy some alone time. But female cardinals sing right along with the males to let the whole world know that they are in charge of the area.

There seems to be some evidence that cardinals do indeed spend the entire year with the same partner. But saying they mate for life gives us the impression that they spend decades of bliss together until they retire to a cardinal condo in Ft. Lauderdale. The fact is a cardinal's life expectancy isn't much longer than a year. So, the cute cardinal couple that has been coming to your feeder for years is probably many different birds. Although there are records of some cardinals having lived more than thirteen years in the wild, they certainly would have had many different mates over that time . . . perhaps even as many as Liz Taylor.

There it is, Dorothy. The answers to your many questions are in that last paragraph, which means you could have ignored all the other blather and just read the final few sentences, like reading a movie review. But if you had skipped to the bottom you would never have learned that cardinals were part of the Red Scare. Yes, even lovely songbirds can harbor dark secrets.

## Being Common Doesn't Make Mallards Any Less Interesting

*Dear Bird Folks:*
*Can you tell me something about my favorite duck, the Mallard? The males are so handsome, yet they act kind of trashy. They are always found in ugly areas, like mud puddles, city parks, and drainage ditches. Is the Mallard an imported bird like the pigeon or starling?*

—*Janet,* FALMOUTH, MA

You know, Janet,

I've been to Falmouth and you are right, there are a lot of handsome but trashy males around there. It must have something to do with all those ships that pull into that seacoast town every day. You are also right about Mallards. They are handsome ducks and yet they are not often admired. Why, I'm not sure. It could have to do with their abundance or it could be their choice of hangouts. It really is hard to warm up to a bird that spends its life in a drainage ditch.

Mallards, without a doubt, are the most successful species of duck ever to hatch out of an egg. They are found in just about every corner of the world. It is thought that several other species of wild ducks have descended from Mallards and that just about all domestic ducks are a direct result of man's breeding of Mallards. The white barnyard ducks, the *Make Way for Ducklings* family, the headless ducks that come with orange sauce, and even Donald and Daisy, Daffy, Huey, Dewey, and Louie, and all the McDucks are related to Mallards. As you can imagine, having so many relatives can lead to problems, and the problems with Mallards are many. But first we should talk about how beautiful and interesting Mallards are. There will be plenty of room to write nasty things about them later.

With its stately green head, the drake Mallard is the classic wild duck. The average person anywhere in the world might not know what a Canvasback or a Bufflehead is, but everybody knows what a Mallard is and what it looks like. It would be hard to find a pond, bog, or marsh that doesn't have a pair of Mallards floating on it. Because they are often found in pairs, many people think that Mallards mate for life. As it turns out, mated pairs go their separate ways after the breeding season. They have one batch of kids and then it's time to move on.

But the newly divorced ducks can't handle eating Swanson's TV Dinner for One for too long. After a month or so hanging out at the singles swamp, they are all paired up again. While most birds pair up in the spring, Mallards begin courting in the fall. By the end of Homecoming Dance, they already know who they'll be spending the winter with, who they'll be mating with in May, and who they'll be taking to divorce court come July.

Now, before you all start blaming the drake Mallard for the breakup, keep in mind that it's the hen that is hard to live with. The voice of the male is so soft and wimpy, it barely even sounds like a duck. The female Mallard's voice is that loud "QUACK, QUACK, QUACK," which is stereotypical of a duck and so hard to live with. After one season of listening to that grating voice, the drake has had enough . . . for a while.

Mallards are known as dabbling ducks. They don't dive under-water, like loons or mergansers, to chase fish. They forage for food by dipping their heads underwater, while their cute little duck bums (Mallards have the best, not to mention original, DA) stick up high in the air. Ninety percent of what they eat is vegeta-tion, but they will also take insects and worms. Other things they will eat are bread, cookies, and Fritos, and that is part of the Mallard's problem.

True wild Mallards are hardy, wary birds that have no use for people and their handouts. They are strong flyers reaching flight speeds of over fifty miles per hour. When startled, they are able to burst straight out of the water like a missile, without having to run along the water to become airborne like many sea ducks do. For a Mallard, there is none of that silly running and flapping just to fly away. They are up, out, and away in seconds. There will be plenty of quacking though. Gotta have that.

The problem with Mallards is that not all of them are truly wild. Mallards are easy to breed in captivity. For years people have raised them for food, as pets, or to kill with guns. And, of course, many of the ducks, hoping to avoid the roasting pan, went AWOL the minute no one was looking. These escapees, called feral, do not have the migration instincts that wild ducks have. Even when winter moves in, they don't go far; they just hang around looking for open water and whatever food they can find.

Most feral ducks that avoided the oven ended up being meals for truly wild predators. Yet, somehow some survived to breed in the spring. These are the "drainage ditch" ducks you mentioned, the trashy birds that will stalk you while you try to picnic in the park. They are the ducks that cause pollution by coming to the same beach every day to beg food from well-meaning people. These also are the ducks that are happy to crossbreed with just about any other species of duck, thus creating an odd creature that looks more like its father was Stephen King than a mallard.

There is another more serious problem that Mallards have caused in recent years. Like the situation above, this problem is also related to humans altering the balance; only this time it's the wild Mallards and not the feral Mallards causing the problems. Changes to the traditional breeding grounds have resulted in wild Mallards moving into the breeding grounds of the American Black Duck and this could possibly mean the end of the Black Duck.

Black Ducks are common on Cape Cod and are still found throughout much of eastern North America. Both the male and the female Black Duck are generic looking brown birds that resemble the female Mallard. Without splashy colors, Black Ducks are largely ignored by most people who don't hunt.

Days ago, when I started this endless Mallard harangue, I mentioned that many species of wild ducks may be direct descendants of Mallards. Black Ducks seem to be one of those species. Being closely related has led to interbreeding. When drake Mallards move into an area, they easily compete with the duller male Black Ducks. One look at the Mallards' flashy green heads and sly smile, and the Black Duck babes are all over them.

Usually when different species interbreed, their freaky-looking offspring are sterile and that is the end of that. But Black Ducks and Mallards are so closely related that their kids are totally fertile and ready to breed with the best of them. And since there are many more Mallards than Black Ducks, the Mallards could slowly be displacing the Black Ducks throughout their entire range.

I like Mallards, too. Whatever is going on, good or bad, the fault is not with the Mallards. Those who changed the ecosystem are, once again, to blame.

Sorry this answer was so long, Janet (is your name still Janet?), and at times got a little dry. I don't know about you, but I could use something to wash down all this boring talk. Perhaps a nice glass of Cold Duck.

## Wood Ducks Might Come to Your Birdhouse Someday

*Dear Bird Folks:*
*I was watching a nature show last week and it had a segment on Wood Ducks. I was shocked at how beautiful these ducks are. I would love to see some. Do we ever get Wood Ducks around here and if so, where could I find some?*

—*Jackie,* BOURNE, MA

Right now, Jackie?

With all of the colorful songbirds returning from the tropics, do we really have to talk about ducks now? We are in the middle of spring, a long overdue spring at that. Can't duck talk wait until fall? No, I suppose you are right. Wood Ducks breed here on Cape Cod and they are just as important as the cutesy songbirds. And besides, what kind of spring would it be without seeing a family of baby ducks? Let's do it!

First of all, if anyone doesn't know what a male Wood Duck looks like, go to the nearest bird book and look at a picture of one. Go ahead, do it now and get ready to be impressed. The drake Wood Duck is without question the most ornate water bird in North America and perhaps the world. It looks less like a duck and more like a clown who has fallen off the back of a bus heading to Vegas. This crazy bird is made up of just about every color you can think of: red, green, orange, tan, white, yellow, black, bright blue, and I think there is some argyle in there, too. The bill alone contains at least four colors and sometimes more on weekends. Yet, this outrageous-looking duck is content to make its home on sedate Cape Cod (and not only in wacky Provincetown either).

The future seems bright for the Wood Duck, but in the early nineteen hundreds it was well on its way to extinction. Back then, many people apparently thought this beautiful bird looked much better dead than flying free and millions of them were shot. Adding to its plight was the loss of its woodland swamps and bottomlands. (That's right, there really is such a thing as bottomland or at least there used to be.) With protection, the Wood Duck has rebounded nicely.

Finding Wood Ducks can be tricky. As their name implies, this duck likes woods and it also can be quite shy. You are more likely to find them on some scummy backwater pond than on a crystal clear lake. The best place to look for them is at a National Wildlife Refuge. Most refuges with appropriate habitat have set out Wood Duck nest boxes. Two great places in Massachusetts are the Great Meadows and Oxbow National Wildlife Refuges. They have put out nesting boxes in which hundreds of baby ducks hatch out each year.

In fact, it is nesting boxes that have helped save the Wood Ducks. Woodies are one of the few ducks that nest off the ground in tree cavities (like woodpeckers and bluebirds). And just like with bluebirds, if you put out a properly built nest box and live near a quiet pond, you too could end up with a nest of Wood Ducks. How cool would that be?

The story of how the young ducks enter the world is yet another amazing chapter from the world of nature. The hen lays about a dozen eggs in a box or tree cavity, which often can be as much as fifty feet above the ground. The mother duck somehow works it out so all the babies hatch at the same time. The next day, when the young birds are barely twenty-four hours old, the mother leaves. Not wanting to be left alone, the ducklings follow her. But the joke is on the kids since the mother can fly and they can't. Off they step into midair, dropping all fifty feet straight down. Somehow they are able to flutter down to earth safely, where they scramble to their feet and quickly march to the nearest scummy pond.

Mid- to late May is the best time to look for Wood Ducks. Once the females start sitting on the eggs, the handsome males drift away and begin to molt. By mid-July, they have lost their signature colors and become rather dull. There's no sense looking for them then, Jackie. With all the political talk shows on TV, you don't need to see any more dull males.

## Hungry Baby Marsh Hawks

*Dear Bird Folks:*

*Do you make house calls? I'm wondering if you would come here to Skaket Marsh and teach a poor baby Marsh Hawk to forage for itself. It has been soaring around for days, giving the most heartrending cries, hoping to be fed.*

*—Nina of Skaket,* ORLEANS, MA

Yo, Nina of Skaket,

Is there some kind of royal family living in Orleans I don't know about? How did you get the title "Nina of Skaket?" Are you related to the King of Prussia or the Duke of Ellington? Sorry, but I stopped making house calls ever since I was ambushed by a mob of hungry gray squirrels back in '95 when I was delivering birdseed.

As their name suggests, Marsh Hawks are birds of prey and are most often found near open fields or marshes. The name "Marsh Hawk" fit them so perfectly that, of course, it had to be changed, and so a few years back their common name was changed to Northern Harrier, just to bug us.

Harriers are wonderful birds for beginning birders. Both their markings and their behavior set them apart from most other hawks, making them easy to identify. Harriers don't hunt for food by sitting and staring like those crusty Red-tailed Hawks we see perched along the interstate. Harriers hunt by flying low to the ground. They glide just above the marsh, with their wings held in a V shape, much like a soaring Turkey Vulture.

Harriers, which spend most of their day hunting on the wing, fly low and actually listen for prey. They have excellent hearing and can instantly react to the rustle or squeaks of mice and meadow voles, their meal of choice (although they will also eat birds and rabbits). Harriers have ear holes that are much larger than those of most hawks. They also have a facial disk of feathers, much like owls, to help direct sounds to their ears. Upon hearing a squeak or rustle, the harrier will drop down for a strike or perhaps stop in midair and briefly hover in an effort to locate prey.

In addition to their hunting behavior, harriers also have a classic field mark that makes identification easy. They have a bright white patch at the base of their tail, giving them the look of a giant flicker or a flying rabbit. Females have a speckled belly and a brown back; the smaller males are mostly gray. The immature of both sexes are also brown on the back, but have a warm pumpkin-colored chest and belly.

Due to their love of open fields and marshes, harriers don't build their nests in trees like other hawks. Instead, they adapted to nesting on the ground. Harrier nests can be found in isolated fields and moorlands, or on the edges of marshes.

While the male harrier hunts for food, the female protects the young. When the male returns with a meal, the female flies out to meet him. Not wanting to have to deal with the kids any more than he has to, the male simply drops the food in midair and keeps going. The female then snatches the mouse-flavored Happy Meal from the sky and returns to the nest.

Here is an odd behavior: When food is plentiful, a male harrier may have a small harem and may mate with as many as four females. That's right, four. What is he thinking? And, believe it or not, he will provide food for all four nest sites at the same time. No wonder the males are gray . . . stress will do that to you every time.

While the young of some bird species are able to feed themselves as soon as they hatch out and others take a few weeks to learn the trick, birds of prey can take months to develop hunting skills. Capturing a speeding rabbit or finding a meadow vole hidden in the deep grass takes a lot more skill than picking a worm off the road. Young hawks and owls need to spend a lot of time watching, learning, and practicing before they can fend for themselves. So, how do they keep from starving in the meantime? They beg.

Like a five-year-old kid in a candy store, begging comes naturally to them. It doesn't need to be learned or practiced and it works great. With the possible exception of the five-year-old, birds are the best beggars in the animal kingdom. And birds of prey, especially owls, are the most skilled beggars of them all. All summer long we get calls from vacationers wanting to know what that awful scream is they hear in the middle of the night. Probably 90 percent of the time those awful screams are the sounds of young Great Horned Owls begging for a nice skunk or a fresh hunk of cat to eat. The other 10 percent of the screams are from the beachgoers applying Solarcaine on yet another sunburn. They never learn.

I'm glad you have young harriers in your marsh, Nina. It's cool they are nesting so close by. Sorry to say that you are just going to have to put up with the begging calls a little while longer. Sooner or later, the young hawks will figure out this hunting thing and finally shut up. In the meantime, either ride it out or go get yourself a sunburn and annoy the hawks with your own screams.

## Nuthatch Nesting Behavior Is
## Strange but Fun to Watch

*Dear Bird Folks:*

*Last week I was thrilled to discover a pair of White-breasted Nuthatches nesting in the birdhouse in my backyard. Yesterday I noticed that the male nuthatch seemed to have something wrong with its beak. He was constantly scraping his long beak across the top of the birdhouse as if there was something on it, much like a person trying to rub a hunk of gum off the bottom of a shoe. Today the bird was again doing the same thing. I'm worried that he needs help getting that gum, pinesap, or whatever off his beak. Is there something wrong?*

—*Tommy,* ROSEWOOD, KY

It's okay, Tommy,

Your nuthatch is fine; he has nothing stuck in his beak. Here is what I think is going on. Even though Kentucky is a "red" state, most White-breasted Nuthatches are diehard Democrats. The bird you saw was simply trying to get the bitter taste of a lost election out of its mouth. Don't worry. He'll get over it . . . eventually.

Lucky you, Tommy, for getting White-breasted Nuthatches to nest in your yard. They are one of the most entertaining of our cavity-nesting birds. Some birds, like Black-capped Chickadees for example, barely let their presence be known. Usually they don't hang out around the outside of their nest box but instead fly directly inside the birdhouse, without even knocking first. I love chickadees but they are boring nesters. Some people don't even realize that the box has been used until later, when they open it and find an old nest and an unpaid cable bill.

White-breasted Nuthatches are showboat tenants. They are constantly crawling all over the outside of the box, looking as if they have forgotten where the entrance hole is. Instead of zipping into the hole in full flight, chickadee-style, they often land on the attached tree and work their way down to the box and eventually into the nest. The chickadee is fairly quiet around the nest site but the nuthatch won't shut up. Their "yank, yank, yank" call is constant, even when they are alone. They never seem to stop muttering to themselves, as if they can't figure out what to do next. See, I told you they were Democrats.

One of the White-breasted Nuthatch's odder nest site behaviors is called "bill sweeping" or, as you called it, "rubbing a hunk of gum off a shoe." Either of the pair, or sometimes both, will sweep their bills back and forth around the nesting area, particularly around the entrance hole. The bird may often have a crushed insect or piece of animal fur in its beak while it is sweeping.

You may ask, "Fine, but why—and what's up with the dead stuff?" Good question. Bill sweeping is something the eggheads with the clipboards have been working on for some time. At this point they really don't know why, and that bugs the heck out them. The best they can come up with is that rubbing dead insects or bits of fur around the entrance hole leaves odors that somehow mask the bird's own scent, and thus protects the nest site from nuthatch-sniffing predators.

I guess that's possible but the last time I checked, insects and small furry animals were pretty high on most predators' menus. Why would those smells keep anything away? The explanation for bill sweeping could be as simple as the bird has a funky song stuck in its head and needs to finish grooving to it before it settles into the nest. Or, in the case of your male bird, Tommy, he could have a little something "on the side" and he is merely wiping off the incriminating ruby-red beak gloss before his old lady catches him.

Whether bill sweeping is understood or not, nuthatches are nevertheless fun birds to observe. What separates them from the rest of the pack is their ability to walk headfirst down a tree trunk. Chickadees, cardinals, robins, and you-name-the-bird can't walk headfirst down a tree. Even woodpeckers, the most tree-dependent birds of all, can't do it. Birds typically keep their feet together, making headfirst balance difficult. But nuthatches spread their feet apart, front to back, like surfer dudes, thus giving them excellent balance and gorgeous tans.

Your birds aren't in trouble, Tommy. They are performing a ritual that all White-breasted Nuthatches do at their nest sites. In a few weeks, if all goes well, you could be seeing young nuthatches, too. However, that all could change quickly if your male bird gets caught with ruby-red beak gloss on his beak. Then instead of seeing him walking down a tree trunk, you could see him standing before Judge Judy. Good luck to him.

## Shy Penguins Keep Their Knees Hidden

*Dear Bird Folks:*
*Someone in my office told me that penguins don't have knees.*
*That would explain why they walk the way they do. Is it possible*
*that they really don't have knees?*

—*Elvira,* MONTREAL, QUEBEC, CANADA

Tough one, Elvira,

Your question isn't tough. The problem is that you are from Quebec. I'm worried that I'll have to answer this question in both English and French. That will be difficult because I only had three months of French when I was in junior high school and that was at least ten years ago, maybe more. I'm not sure if I can write this whole thing in French. Heck, sometimes even English is tough for me. Many people don't know it but English is my second language. The problem is I don't have a first language, but I think that's pretty obvious.

Ever since the movie *March of the Penguins* came out, we have been getting a load of penguin questions. Are they really birds? Can they fly? How fast can they swim? What do they eat? Which came first, the penguins or the nuns? But you are the first person to ask about them having knees. It's nice to know that you guys are discussing birds in your office. Here, where our staff is supposed to be talking about birds, the two most frequently asked questions are: "What's for lunch?" and "What's for lunch?" But not always in that order.

The answer to your question is *oui*, of course, penguins have knees. If they didn't have knees, they wouldn't be able to move on land, or lower themselves to sit on their eggs, or play the spoons. Did you ever think of that up there in Montreal?

A penguin's knees are hidden under the bird's feathers, protected from the crazy Antarctic cold. I have to agree that the way penguins waddle along it seems as if they don't have knees, but their silly-looking walk is the result of having very short legs, not from a lack of knees. Of course, being a few pounds on the chunky side doesn't help them with their stride either.

Here's a way to get a sense of what it's like to walk with short penguin legs. While you are there in the office, Elvira, and the boss has gone out for a croissant, take a tennis ball, or in your case a hockey puck, and place it between your knees. Now, try to walk around. You'll be waddling much like a penguin, only without the fishy smell.

Penguins are totally flightless birds. Other flightless birds, like ostriches or emus, have long, powerful legs. Even poor flyers, such as the roadrunner, have legs that can instantly carry them away from danger. Penguins, on the other hand, have legs that seem to be for entertainment purposes only. They are short, stubby, and barely get the job done. But they do get the job done and that's all penguins care about.

It is actually a good thing penguins have short, stubby legs since they are, of course, seabirds. Long legs would only cause drag underwater and slow them down. The birds propel themselves with their flipper-like wings; they use their legs and feet to help with the steering, and that's it.

There is no bird in the world that can match a penguin's swimming ability. The loons, the puffins, the eiders, even SpongeBob, are all in the minor leagues when compared to the masters of the sea. What makes the penguins so good? All of the aforementioned birds are able to fly; their wings still have flight feathers. Penguins decided that if they have to be in the ocean most of their lives, they might as well go for it all and quickly turned their wings into powerful flippers. And by "quickly," I mean over several million years, which is still faster than the response time from FEMA.

Not only are penguins champion swimmers, they are the top divers, too. Most other birds have hollow bones, which keep them light enough to fly, but penguins have solid bones, which help them with their deep dives. Emperor Penguins have been reported to dive as deep as 1,700 feet, which is nearly twice the height of the Empire State Building and over three times the height of the pile of bills on my desk right now.

Thanks for the question, Elvira. Keep talking about birds up there in Montreal. If you ever get to Cape Cod, please stop in for a visit, although we'll all probably be at lunch.

## How to Find Roadrunners

*Dear Bird Folks:*

*My ten-year-old son has always wanted to see a roadrunner. We have set up a family vacation to Arizona, where I understand the roadrunner is the state bird. Do you think that we'll actually see roadrunners? Also, do you have any advice on how we might locate them?*

—*Kenny,* MADISON, WI

Are you kidding, Kenny?

You are setting up your vacation because your ten-year-old wants to see a roadrunner? That's pretty good. When I was ten I wanted to see mermaids but I couldn't convince the rest of the family to take me where I needed to go. Although my father was interested, my mother was having none of it. We ended up at something called Old Sturbridge Village. What a rundown place that was. And there wasn't a mermaid in sight.

I can help you with your roadrunner search, but first you need to know one thing: The roadrunner is the state bird of New Mexico, not Arizona. I know it all seems the same once you get past Iowa and it kind of is, but the New Mexicanians would not be happy if they lost their state bird to Arizona. Remember, the atom bomb was invented in New Mexico. We need to stay on their good side.

The Greater Roadrunner is one freaky bird. It lives in the hottest region of the country, spends most of its life running totally barefoot across the sun-scorched earth, and actually goes out of its way to find snakes. It is unique looking, ranking up there with puffins and ostriches as a bird that everyone can instantly identify. It is found in the arid states of the Southwest, including Arizona, New Mexico, and Texas. They all look the same, except that the birds from Texas have gun racks.

When we think of roadrunners, most people think about how fast they run. At over twenty miles per hour, they do run fast for a bird or any other two-legged creature (except kangaroos, which are rare in Arizona). When hunting or avoiding danger, roadrunners will use their impressive speed, but it's their maneuverability that really makes the difference. Their extra long tail gives them great balance and allows them to make instant course changes. These tricky moves have been a curse to predators—and one coyote in particular.

When at rest, roadrunners sometimes cock their heads and lift their tails straight up, looking like a giant letter V. But when they are running, the tail and neck flatten out and the bird becomes a skinny-legged torpedo blasting through the underbrush. Let's not forget that roadrunners are birds, so they can fly. However, they stink at it, only gliding for short distances before they begin racing like maniacs along the ground again.

Roadrunners are serious carnivores. They eat mice, lizards, and tarantulas and will even leap into the air to snag a humming-bird. They also eat snakes, including the occasional juicy rattler. The birds sometimes hunt in pairs, with one bird distracting the snake while the second bird zips in from behind. The bird's usual MO (that's hip talk for "method of operating") is to grab the snake's head in its beak and then smash it against a rock. The bird then proceeds to swallow the snake, head first. If the snake is too long, the bird will simply let the rest of the reptile dangle from its mouth. It will then go about its daily activities while it waits for digestion to make room. This feeding behavior may sound unique but I've seen my kids do the same thing with spaghetti.

Even though roadrunners are fairly common birds, finding one won't be easy. They don't flock up like crows and blackbirds or hang out at ponds like ducks. Roadrunners set up a territory and rarely leave it. If you cross a territory, the best you can hope to see is one or two birds. My advice is to drive slowly down a quiet, isolated road, roll down your window and listen. If you hear the classic "beep, beep" sound, it isn't a roadrunner; it is most likely the car behind you wanting you to get the heck out of the way. A roadrunner's real call is a low, dovelike cooing; they only make that "beep, beep" sound when the TV cameras are rolling.

In Arizona, you'll probably have better luck searching for them in the southern part of the state. Quiet, secluded chaparrals and arid regions are what roadrunners seem to prefer. Have your binoculars ready to catch a glimpse of these speedy birds. But be careful not to use Acme binoculars. You won't stand a chance with those.

Have a good trip, Kenny. I hope you guys get to see a roadrunner. And even though you'll be in the desert and not near any water, could you keep an eye out for a mermaid for me? I know they're out there somewhere.


## That Old Ostrich Rumor Is Just Plain Stupid

*Dear Bird Folks:*
*What is the true story with ostriches sticking their heads in the sand? Do they really do that or is that just an old wives' tale? Are they really trying to hide or are they looking for something?*
—*A. Rose,* BEND, OR

Hello, A.,

This one is easy. Ostriches don't put their heads in the sand to hide. That would be silly. When ostriches stick their heads in the sand, they are looking for spare change. In fact, ostriches are so good at finding change that in Africa many retired men use ostriches at the beach instead of metal detectors. Ostriches are not only better at finding change than metal detectors, but they don't need batteries or make those annoying beeping sounds.

Ostriches are huge, flightless birds of the open African savanna. They are by far the world's largest birds, standing eight feet high and weighing more than three hundred pounds. That's equivalent to the weight of 1,602 Blue Jays or 48,362 of the burliest Ruby-throated Hummingbirds.

Ostriches are also the world's fastest-running bird. They can reach speeds of forty-five miles per hour, putting them in the same league as the cheetah, the antelope, and my neighbor's Jack Russell terrier who won't let me cut through the yard.

Another cool thing about ostriches is their feet: each foot has only two toes. One toe is small and mostly used for balance; the other is huge, more like a foot, with a two-inch-long claw. With their massive legs and deadly claws, ostriches are capable of delivering kicks that can smash the skull of a would-be predator. Now, that's a pleasant thought.

With such power, speed, and height, ostriches have few natural enemies, except for lightning and low branches. Like most wild things, ostriches were doing quite well until humans got involved. Someone decided that we couldn't live without an ostrich feather sticking out of our hats and thousands of ostriches were killed so we could have this all-important decoration.

Ostriches were well on their way to extinction when somebody figured out that they could be raised on farms. Ostrich farms sprang up all over, providing the world with homegrown ostrich parts and the wild birds were saved. However, I'm sure that the birds living on the farms aren't too thrilled with this new arrangement.

So where did the notion of ostriches putting their heads in the sand come from? Ostriches live in the open savanna where there are few places to hide. When an ostrich wants to go undetected, it drops its head and long neck to the ground in hopes of fooling a predator into thinking that it is a distant bush. It also must have fooled some delirious sunstroked folks into thinking its head was totally buried.

Ostriches are pretty interesting birds, but the idea of sticking their heads in the sand is definitely an old wives' tale. And while I'm on the subject of wives' tales, you should know that you don't get warts from toads, you don't have to wait an hour after you eat before swimming, and dogs' mouths are not clean. And I mean any dog's mouth, especially my neighbor's foul-mouthed Jack Russell terrier.

## Yes, Flamingos Are Really Real

*Dear Bird Folks:*
*I know flamingos are real birds, but do they really exist in the wild or are they just an odd bird that zoos have created? And is there some secret reason why people have plastic ones in their yards?*

—*Dora,* BARNSTABLE, MA

First of all, Dora,

Zoos do not invent their own birds. Dr. Seuss is the only one allowed to do that. Zoos have real birds. They may not be happy birds but they are definitely real. Flamingos are truly wild birds that can be found in many pockets of the world, including Africa, India, the Caribbean, South America, Mexico, the Galapagos and, of course, any trailer park. Flamingos can also be found in parts of Florida. In fact, flamingos have been around for over seven million years, which makes them younger than most of Florida's residents.

Many of the Florida birds are escapees from parks and reserves. Back in the nineteen thirties, in what can only be described as one of the stupidest moves of the century, some bonehead captured a flock of flamingos in Central America and released them at the Hialeah Race Track in Miami. The next day all the birds flew away. Duh! A few years later, they tried it again, only this time they clipped the birds' flight feathers and a colony of nine hundred flamingos is there to this day.

Flamingos are unique birds. They are as tall as a Great Blue Heron, only wicked thin, like a supermodel. Being thin and frail makes flamingos basically defenseless. To protect their young, they nest in large colonies in the middle of alkaline or saline lakes and lagoons that are so gross even predators won't go in there. They build tall mud nests, which look like top hats, to keep their eggs out of the water.

The flamingos' feeding behavior is among the most unusual in the bird world. A flamingo takes its wide, hook-shaped bill and sweeps it back and forth along the bottom of a lake or bay. As it sweeps, the bird sucks up as much bottom pond scum as it can get. Then acting more like a humpback whale than a bird, the flamingo forces the gooey water out through tiny comb-like teeth on the edges of its bill, trapping the algae and tiny marine creatures that make up the bulk of its diet. This daily meal of pond scum probably explains how the birds stay so thin.

Back in the 1950s, when a trip to Florida was quite costly and not yet an annual requirement, Florida souvenirs became status symbols. To capitalize on this bizarre trend, a company in Leominster, Massachusetts, Union Plastics, hired a sculptor to create a flamingo lawn ornament. A twenty-one-year-old designer named Don Featherstone (no, I am not kidding) was given the job and the plastic pink flamingo was born. The timing was perfect because Americans were moving to the suburbs and needed something to add color to the green desert they called a lawn.

Then came the rebellious sixties and flamingos quickly went from status to tacky and then disappeared from the landscape. The late seventies and early eighties ushered in the tasteless disco era and suddenly tacky was back in style. The TV show *Miami Vice* helped push flamingos onto the front page once again. Flamingo items are still popular, although most people buy them not to enjoy, but to annoy. Either way is fine by me.

It should be noted, Dora, that the original plastic flamingos have Don Featherstone's signature under the tail. If you want to know if the flamingos in your neighbor's yard are originals, sneak over some night with a flashlight and peek under a bird's tail. Just be sure to have a good story ready because you know you are going to get caught by the cops.

## Ospreys Are Everywhere and They're All Identical

*Dear Bird Folks:*
*While on a bus tour in Great Britain this spring, I saw what I'm sure was an Osprey flying overhead. I was shocked. What was one of our beautiful birds of prey doing in Scotland?*

—*Alex,* DENNIS PORT, MA

Living, Alex,
That is what the Osprey you saw was doing in Scotland. It was living. Ospreys love Scotland. They arrive there every spring to feed on wild haggis.

"Our" Osprey is one of the most widely distributed birds in the world. They can be found just about everywhere there are fish, including Europe, India, Asia, Japan, and Australia. In fact, the only places where you won't find Ospreys are Antarctica and certain neighborhoods in Detroit.

A unique thing about Ospreys is that they are a family of one. That's all one species worldwide. That's impressive. The hummingbird family, for example, has hundreds of different species. There are more than three hundred hummingbirds of assorted sizes, shapes and colors, but only one style of Osprey. There are no "Great Ospreys" living in the Alps or "Bow-legged Ospreys" living on the beach in Malibu. Whether you are seeing an Osprey in Dennis Port or on your next bus tour to the jungles of New Guinea, they are all basically the same bird. Evidently, they got it right the first time and evolution didn't need to make changes.

The Ospreys in our area were almost wiped out thirty years ago due to the overuse of DDT. As we know by now, DDT prevents the birds from producing calcium. Since eggs are made of nearly 100 percent calcium, their eggs were often laid soft or broken. In 1973, when DDT was finally banned in this country, there were only ten nesting Ospreys in Massachusetts. The ban on DDT, along with the heroic efforts of Jo and Gil Fernandez of Westport, Massachusetts, helped the Osprey make a major recovery. Other similar projects throughout their North American range have also had success. The Massachusetts population of Ospreys has jumped from ten pairs in 1973 to nearly four hundred nesting pairs today. Now there are nearly as many Osprey nests in Massachusetts as there are Dunkin' Donuts, only the Ospreys produce a lot less litter.

Ospreys subsist almost entirely on live fish. It is the only raptor that plunges into the water, much like a kingfisher. However, the Osprey doesn't grab fish in its beak like other diving birds; it dives in feet first, grabbing the fish with its powerful talons. Ospreys have an unusual fourth toe that can move front-to-back to help them grab the fish. In addition to that weird fourth toe, they also have rough scales on their feet to help hold onto the slippery fish. Once airborne with the fish, the Osprey will often maneuver the fish so its head faces forward. It is believed that having the fish facing forward makes it more aerodynamic for flying, plus it allows the fish to enjoy the view.

Most of us know Ospreys from the huge stick nests they build. Historically, Ospreys have nested on the tops of dead trees but like the Barn Swallows, Ospreys have found a way to exploit man and his structures. Ospreys now build their massive nests on everything from utility poles to water towers. However, the artificial nesting platforms pioneered by those Fernandez people are what has really helped bring the birds back.

I agree with you, Alex; Ospreys are beautiful birds of prey. And even though they are creatures of the world and not truly "ours," many people in our area should be proud of the efforts they have made in bringing this wonderful bird back from the brink. Without them the Osprey might have gone the way of the dinosaur, the Passenger Pigeon, and ice cream cones that cost less than five dollars.

## A Flock of Turkeys Does Not a Family Make

*Dear Bird Folks:*
*We have a family of turkeys coming to our yard. Recently two males have been fanning out their tails, but the females seem to ignore them and never fan their tails. Is the male turkey the only one that fans out its tail feathers?*

*—Eileen,* HOPKINTON, MA

No kidding, Eileen,

Hopkinton? My sister lives in Hopkinton. Do you know her? She is kind of like me but she looks quite a bit older. Evidently, it's a hard life out there in Hopkinton. That is pretty neat how you have a flock of turkeys in your yard, though. I don't think they can actually be called a "family" since these birds are trying to mate with each other and, except for certain parts of the country, mating with family members is not encouraged.

For most of the year turkeys can be found in one of four different kinds of flocks. Mature males (toms) hang out together and have little to do with the females or the kids. Mature females (hens) who either didn't successfully mate or have lost their brood also form a flock. These spinsters wander the countryside feeding and talking about how rotten men are. The third flock is a true family, consisting of the mother hen and her offspring. As the mother hen's young males (jakes) get older, they leave her flock and join up with a fourth flock made up of other jakes. Jakes are the young hotties of the turkey world. They hang out together, just counting down the days until they become adults (toms), which takes about two years.

When spring arrives, the length of day, combined with improving weather, causes the turkeys' hormones to kick into breeding mode. The toms gobble in an effort to attract the hens. Once the two flocks find each other, the toms start showing off. Like you said, the males fan out their tails, fluff out their feathers, and strut around like John Travolta in *Saturday Night Fever.*

The turkey world is more sophisticated than you might think. The meeting of the two groups doesn't turn into some kind of wild orgy. The dominant male is the first to mate. The other toms only mate when the dominant male is "occupied." The hens, on the other hand, are not bullied into this mating ritual and only breed at a time of their choosing or when they are in the mood, just like most females.

After mating, each hen leaves the group to find a secret location to lay her eggs. One egg is laid each day until the entire clutch of ten to twelve eggs is complete. Only after all the eggs are laid will the female begin to incubate her eggs. It's important for all the eggs to hatch within a day or so. Newly hatched turkeys are "precocial," which means they hatch out covered in feathers, with their eyes open, and ready to rock and roll. If all the chicks didn't hatch out at once, the mother would have trouble controlling and protecting the moving chicks while she continued to brood her unhatched eggs.

A mother turkey protects her young family from predators and weather, but her chicks feed themselves. Insects are the first food they choose. Soft, protein-rich insects help the young birds grow rapidly. After a few months of chowing on bugs, the growing turkeys move into their teenage phase and start eating seeds, fruit, acorns, and, of course, French fries and nachos. Eventually, her young males will be old enough to move out and join other jakes of the 'hood.

It's good to know you have turkeys, Eileen. I'm sure they are one of the few highlights of living in Hopkinton. If you happen to see my sister, wish her a happy birthday for me. It will save me from having to send her a card.

## The Great Auk: Something Else We Messed Up

*Dear Bird Folks:*
*I have been seeing posters around announcing a program enti-*
*tled "The Spirit of the Great Auk." The posters made me laugh.*
*Aren't Great Auks those real stupid birds that people used to*
*make fun of? Why would there be a program about the "spirit" of*
*such a stupid bird?*

*—Jim, EASTHAM, MA*

Hang on, Jimbo,
I'm sure I have mentioned this at least one other time, but with the exception of our brain-dead barnyard poultry, there are

no "stupid" birds. Any creature that can build a nest or catch fish by just using its face has to have some brainpower. And just so you know, the program is about the Great Auk. The "stupid bird" you are thinking about is the Dodo bird. By the way, Dodos weren't stupid either; they just had poor study habits.

The history of the Great Auk is interesting but a bit sad toward the end, so you might want to refill your Prozac if you plan to read on.

Although most of us are unfamiliar with them, auks are extremely abundant seabirds. They are typically black and white, found in the ocean, look ducklike on the water, and only come on land to breed. They walk like drunks and are shaky flyers, but are wicked good swimmers, using their wings to "fly" underwater. The puffin, with its odd punk-rock-looking bill, is the most recognizable of all the auks.

Auks' legs and feet are positioned closer to their tail so they are able to stand straight up, like a person. This is where the Great Auks stood out from the crowd. The Great Auk didn't earn the name "great" because of any significant accomplishment, but because of its size. Standing nearly two-and-a-half feet high, the Great Auk towered over other auks. A Great Auk basketball team would have easily dominated the other seabird teams. Unfortunately, Great Auks had fouled out permanently just before basketball was invented.

Compared to its gigantic body size, the bird had such ridiculously small wings that there was no way it could fly. But the Great Auk wasn't upset; it knew it was a superior swimmer. It could easily catch all the food it needed, had very few predators, and didn't smack into windows like the flying birds do. Things were going along fabulously for North America's only flightless bird until . . . stop me if you've heard this before . . . along came those wacky Europeans, who messed things up.

Years ago, when the Europeans had more on their minds than worrying about the price of the euro, they would explore the world looking for things to eat. Early European fishermen (I think it really was all men in those days) took full advantage of the juicy, flightless auks. They would simply pull up to a nesting colony, herd thousands of defenseless birds onto the ship, and turn them into auk cutlets. In a sad but typical show of shortsightedness, adult birds were eaten, their young were used as fish bait, and their eggs were scrambled or thrown at passing Viking ships on Halloween.

Great Auks mostly bred in the North Atlantic and could be found wintering off the coast of Cape Cod. One major nesting colony was near Newfoundland, on a place called Funk Island. Funk Island, of course, was named for those awesome parties the birds had before the Europeans came.

By 1844, only two Great Auks and one egg remained on the entire planet (on Eldey Island in Iceland, if you must know). In keeping with tradition, once discovered, those final two birds were killed for European collectors, and the last egg was smashed. The Great Auk was no more.

The Great Auk was truly a unique bird, Jim, and its loss has left a void. But it should not be confused with the Dodo. And the Dodo should not be confused with anything that is stupid. We all know who deserves the title of stupid.

## Jumbo Woodpecker Mystery

*Dear Bird Folks:*

*My husband keeps trying to convince me that the huge woodpeck-er on our property is one of those rare Ivory-billed Woodpeckers, and not a Pileated Woodpecker. I think he's crazy, but the two birds do look fairly similar in the book. Could you tell me the dif-ference between them? And while you are at it, please tell me a lit-tle about the habits of the Pileated Woodpecker.*

*—Janice,* COOPERSTOWN, NY

That's familiar, Janice,

Your last line, "And while you are at it . . . ," reminds me of the phrase I hear a lot at my house, only here it's "While you're up . . ." The people in my house would rather do without something than actually get it themselves. This is what I hear: "While you're up, could you get me a napkin . . . and perhaps a glass of milk . . . plus a slice of pie . . . with a scoop of ice cream, vanilla. Oh, and don't forget to heat the pie." Whether it's "while you are at it" or "while you are up," either one means more work, and less pie, for me. But I don't mind doing the extra work for you, Janice. Just don't ask me for a napkin.

I'm a bit at a disadvantage trying to explain the differences between the two giant woodpeckers because I've never seen an Ivory-billed Woodpecker. Few people have actually seen one alive, other than one or two lucky researchers, and your crazy husband. This is just a guess, but I think a big difference between the two is that one bird has an "ivory bill." Another thing to look for is the color of the bird's back. When clinging to a tree trunk, woodpecker-style, the Ivory-bill has a lot of white on its back, while the Pileated's back is all black. Also the Ivory-bill's chin is black, while the Pileated's chin is white, just like Santa's. In addition, the Ivory-bill is a considerably larger bird (19 inches) than the Pileated (16 inches). Have your husband run outside with a yardstick the next time you see the bird in question. That would be helpful.

It is highly unlikely that anyone reading this will ever see an Ivory-billed Woodpecker, but with a little effort, any of us can find the somewhat similar-looking Pileated Woodpecker. The Pileated is far more adaptive than the Ivory-bill and has been able to turn the misery created by human encroachment into an opportunity. While the Pileated actually likes us and will sometimes come to our feeders and backyards, humans have driven the Ivory-bill into possible extinction. (In case you somehow missed the saga, for the first time in over sixty years there has been a reliable sighting of the once-thought-to-be-extinct Ivory-billed Woodpecker. Yea! However, as of now, the eggheads can't seem to agree on whether the bird that was seen was indeed an Ivory-bill or merely a Pileated Woodpecker that likes to dress up to look like one. Stay tuned.)

One of the first signs that a Pileated is in your area is the hole that it leaves behind in trees. Most woodpeckers make cute, round, cookie-cutter nest holes. A Pileated's hole, however, is anything but perfectly round and looks as if it was made by a blindfolded drunk wielding a fire ax. When digging out insects from deep inside a tree, this woodpecker digs massive rectangle-shaped holes, which make the tree look like it went through the Battle of Gettysburg.

If you think that digging such large holes could cause significant damage to the trees, you are right. Of course it does. But the birds usually aren't interested in healthy trees; they are more attracted to dead or dying trees, which are filled with lovely wood-boring insects. Woodpeckers slam their huge chisel-shaped bills against the sides of trees and when they find a spot that sounds hollow from insect damage, they start hacking their way in. When a Pileated Woodpecker decides it wants to get inside a tree, it is not delicate about it and as a result, the area around the tree is filled with hunks of flying bark and wood chips, and pieces of any unlucky squirrel that gets in the way.

If you have Pileated Woodpeckers on your property now, you will probably have them for a long time. Pileateds, some of which may live ten years or more, don't migrate and usually spend most of their lives in the same vicinity. They only require large trees to keep them happy. People who live in an area with those puny ornamental trees are unlikely ever to have a Pileated Woodpecker come for a visit.

A freakish problem that occasionally plagues these woodpeckers is lightning. The large trees that attract the birds also attract lightning bolts. Many woodpeckers are lost when a summer storm hits and they don't get out of the bathtub in time.

Your husband is not really crazy, Janice, but the only way he is going to see an Ivory-billed Woodpecker in Cooperstown is if one is inducted into the Baseball Hall of Fame. That, of course, is silly. Although the rare woodpecker still has a better chance of being inducted than Pete Rose does.

# 4.

## Stuff . . . and What to Do with It

The good news is bird watching is more popular than ever. The bad news is there are tons of new birding products on the market. You'd think a lot of new products would be a positive thing. And you would be right if all the new products were any good, but we all know better than that. I'm not saying there are crooks out there, because who needs the lawsuits? However, in the rush to get things to market some items aren't what they could be. One well-known feeder manufacturer once told me, "We don't have time to test everything we make." That was comforting to hear (add your own level of sarcasm). There doesn't have to be a lot of equipment involved in backyard bird watching. You need a feeder, a bird book, a pair of binoculars, and perhaps a birdbath if you live in a dirty neighborhood. That's about it. And if you buy the right products the first time, you won't have to buy them again, ever.

## Good Looks Aren't Everything When It Comes to Feeders

*Dear Bird Folks:*
*I want to buy my parents a bird feeder for Christmas, but I found myself totally confused by the conflicting selection at my local garden center. The clerk was friendly, but just as clueless about the feeders as I was. My wife suggested I write to those Cape Cod bird people for feeder advice. Any suggestions on which feeder I should buy my folks?*

—*Stewart,* THOMPSON, CT

Swell, Stewart, just swell,

Not only do I have the huge task of choosing the proper Christmas gifts for the people on my list, now I have the added pressure of selecting what you should get for your family in Connecticut. And all because your local garden center is run by friendly, dumb people. Why can't you just write a letter to Santa like everyone else? Santa never makes mistakes. Well, except for that time he brought me Elmo underwear. I don't know what went wrong that year.

There are a lot of really good feeders out there, Stewart, but in fairness to you and the friendly clerk, there are a lot of stink bombs, too. It's easy to be fooled by the ones with all the artsy bling-bling on them, but a good rule of thumb is: When it comes to bird feeders, the uglier the better. Bird feeders and guard dogs need to look downright ugly to get the job done. A bird feeder in the shape of a church, a castle, or Graceland isn't going to make it through many New England winters . . . just like a Peke-a-poo isn't going to keep many bad guys from stealing the gold you have hidden under your bed, even if you do take the bow out of its hair.

When I say ugly, I don't mean it has to look like a gargoyle or an NHL hockey player, but it can't have cutesy flowers on it either.

A good feeder should be all about lasting for years and not about driving up your property value. I find the best feeders are made in this country and not overseas. I have no issues with imported products but unlike cameras and TVs, right now the best bird feeders are built here.

Any good feeder must be easy to fill but more importantly, easy to clean. A good feeder is made to come apart easily so you can remove any old or wet seed. If you can't figure out how to clean the feeder, don't buy it. Many people are attracted to feeders with large capacities, so they won't have to fill them as frequently. That can be a mistake. Often, seed will get wet and spoil before it can all be eaten. Several small feeders might be a better choice than one extra-large one. Also, birds are only protected by a thin layer of feathers so avoid feeders with sharp metal or glass.

Wooden feeders appeal to many people and if taken care of, they will last. But often, wooden feeders will be chewed up. If you buy a wooden feeder, you'll need to protect it from squirrels, raccoons, and most importantly, beavers.

If you are going to buy your folks only one feeder, Stewart, I suggest a tube-style feeder. Tube feeders are usually three or four inches around and eighteen inches tall, clear, with metal on the cover, metal perches (no, the bird's feet won't stick in the winter), and metal on other key points to keep mammals from chewing them up. Good tube feeders are easy to fill, easy to clean, keep the seed reasonably dry, and with baffles, are easy to squirrel-proof. Tube feeders cost between twenty and thirty bucks, and most have a lifetime warranty.

I know what you are thinking. This all sounds good, but twenty or thirty bucks is a lot to spend for a Christmas present, especially when it's only for your parents. Maybe you could get some other siblings to chip in. If not, then forget the whole thing and buy them a set of Elmo underwear. I'll sell you mine . . . cheap.

## A Little Feeder Maintenance
## Won't Kill You

*Dear Bird Folks:*
*This wet spring has my bird feeders looking a little grungy. Any*
*thoughts on how and when to clean bird feeders?*
                              *—Paul,* PROVINCETOWN, MA

Now, Paul.

You should clean your feeders *now.* I said "now," even before
you finish reading this. Stand up, open the door, walk outside,
and take your feeders in. Go ahead, I'll wait . . . still waiting . . .
Did you do it? Okay, good. Now take them completely apart. All
well-designed feeders should easily come apart for cleaning. If
your feeders don't come apart for cleaning, fill them with dirt
and plant tomatoes in them.

Next, pour yourself a bucket of hot water; add a bit of bleach.
Dish soap is fine, too, and the bubbles are fun to play with. Place
all your feeder parts in the tub and let them soak for a while—in
your case, Paul, maybe a month or so. After soaking, scrub away
all the goo and scuzziness, rinse well, and let everything dry in the
sun. Finally, if you still remember how, reassemble your feeders,
fill them with fresh seed, and put them back outside for any birds
that haven't already filed a complaint with the board of health.

Now that your feeders are clean, the best way to keep them
clean is to totally empty them every time you go to fill them.
Never, ever put fresh seed on top of old seed or "top off" your
feeder. Ditch the old seed. Don't be so cheap. When you fill
your feeder, dump the old seed on the ground for the doves and
sparrows. Or, if you insist on being cheap, empty the remaining
seed into an empty coffee can. Then add your fresh seed and put
the old seed on top. If the old seed is dry it is okay to rotate it, you
know, like they do with the milk in the grocery store. They put the

old, nasty milk out front and the good, fresh milk in the back. (Of course, we always reach around back for the good milk, but the birds haven't figured that out yet.)

Keeping your feeders clean and your seed fresh is more important than most people realize. Every day customers bring me feeders that need repair, but they don't seem to notice how disgusting their feeders are. I can't imagine what these people are thinking. The shower drains at your local YMCA have less gooey crap in them than what these people are putting food into. We need to remember that a little chickadee, weighing less than half an ounce, is trusting that the food we offer is clean and safe.

Long rainy spells can make keeping feeders clean particularly difficult. During wet weather it's best not to use large feeders, or at least don't fill them completely. Birdseed isn't cheap and if your food gets wet it will spoil and you'll need to throw it in the trash. That's right, not on the ground, in the trash. Moldy seed is dangerous for birds. You can't even throw it over the fence into the neighbor's yard. And if there are moldy seeds or shells on the ground, rake those up, too.

A common mistake is filling a large feeder and then going away. Many "weekenders," who have a real home plus a vacation home, think it is important to keep their feeders filled while they are away. The fact is they may be doing the birds more harm than good. Rotten seed is not safe for birds. If you are not around to maintain your feeders, do the birds a favor and take them in while you are gone. Believe me, the birds will return when you put your feeders out again. They understand that you are rich, have two houses, and are sometimes out of town. It doesn't bother them one bit. Although they do appreciate the occasional postcard.

## Water + Sugar =
## Mold in Hummingbird Feeders

*Dear Bird Folks:*
*I would like to know if there is any way to prevent mildew from*
*forming inside my hummingbird feeders. I try to change the solu-*
*tion often but I still get mildew. Any suggestions? Thank you.*

—*Marie,* MAHOPAC, NY

You're welcome, Marie,

In June of 2000 I started writing answers to questions about birds. At this point, I think I've answered 10,000 questions. Maybe I'm wrong, but 10,000 sounds impressive. However, I'm only exaggerating for your sake, Marie, because whatever the number is, you need to know that you are the only person ever to write "thank you" at the end of the question. I knew that if I hung on long enough, somebody, someday would show me some appreciation. I just never guessed it would be someone from Mahopac. I really should personally deliver a bouquet of flowers, but since I have no idea where the heck Mahopac is, I'll simply say "you're welcome" and save myself some gas money.

Mold (a.k.a. mildew) is a big problem in hummingbird feeders. Evidently, the simple sugar water solution we use in our hummingbird feeders is just right for attracting and growing lovely, black mold. Did you ever do that experiment in high school where you put a few drops of sugar water on a piece of bread and watch mold form? No? Me neither. I was too busy eating the bread, but I do remember watching other kids do it. The purpose of the experiment was to show that mold, which is really a fungus, loves two things: water and food (i.e., the sugar).

Some molds are good. Penicillin, of course, comes from a good mold. Other molds are bad, like the kind that gets into your hummingbird feeder. Still other molds are downright nasty. The worst is the infamous Jell-O mold, the kind with hunks of fruit cocktail in it. Talk about evil. Fortunately, a team of researchers, led by Drs. Ben and Jerry, has found a way to remove that kind of awful mold from the dessert list of civilized society. They may have saved us all.

You are right to be concerned, Marie. Mold in your feeder is not good for the birds. You mentioned that you change the solution "often," but you are still getting mold. The answer, then, would be to change it more often. The rule of thumb is to change it every three days but if that isn't getting the job done, try changing your food every other day. If that doesn't help, try weakening your formula. The stronger the sugar content, the faster the mold can grow.

The most common mixture is four parts water to one part sugar. Some generous people add more sugar and make a three-to-one mixture. That's not a great idea. A richer mixture may cause mold to grow faster and could also lead to an epidemic of hummingbird diabetes.

Many people boil the water before they add the sugar. The thought is that boiling retards the mold growth. That may be a good thing to do, but I've always been too lazy to try. If you aren't a slacker like me, you may want to try boiling and see if that helps. Another thing to try is to move your feeder into the shade. Shade seems to slow mold growth in hummer feeders, which is surprising since most mold loves shade. Go figure.

The flat, saucer-like feeders are the easiest to clean. Removing mold should not be a problem with that style feeder. However, if you are using one of those silly, complicated feeders that looks like a Roman fountain, you may have problems. If you can't reach the mold with any kind of brush, try soaking the feeder in a mild solution of one quarter cup of bleach to a gallon of water. Earthy types often use white vinegar and water (four to one) instead of bleach. After soaking, rinse the feeder thoroughly and pour the remaining vinegar solution over organic greens. It makes a lovely dressing.

I'm glad you wrote in, Marie. Hummingbird feeder maintenance is important. I hear about too many feeders that are left unattended for days or weeks at a time. Once the food has spoiled, the birds will not use it no matter how hungry they are. Some researchers claim that hummers would rather let themselves starve to death than eat spoiled food. Which is exactly how I feel about fruit cocktail mixed into Jell-O mold.

## Put the Feeder Where You Can See It

*Dear Bird Folks:*
*I received a very nice bird feeder as a gift. I have never used one before. Do you have any advice on where I should put my new feeder?*

—*Carl,* ASHLAND, NC

Well, Carl,

My favorite place to put a feeder is outside. A lot of people don't agree with that but they are making a big mistake. Sure, putting your feeder outside means that you may have to go out to fill it once in a while, but that's the chance you'll have to take.

You know, Carl, there are a few people out there thinking, "What a stupid question. What's so hard about putting out a bird feeder?" Well, I for one am glad you asked. First, I'm all out of questions to answer. Second, feeder placement is more important than most people realize. Lots of things should be considered; some are for your benefit, while others are more important for the birds.

If you are like me, you'll think mostly of your own needs first, and well you should. Place your feeder where you can best see it.

If you spend most of your time at the kitchen table, at your desk, or lying on a massage table listening to New Age music like me, then place your feeder so you can view it from those spots. Remember, we feed birds for our own pleasure. It is pretty silly to have a feeder that you never get to see. That would be like buying a stereo without speakers, or eating white chocolate; both are rather pointless.

Also keep in mind that you will need to fill and clean this feeder . . . regularly and often during bad weather. Don't put your feeder in some hard-to-reach place, like the top of a high tree or near an active volcano (Hawaii readers only). You should be able to pick up your feeder, dump out any old seed, and refill it without having to use a ladder. If you do need to fill a feeder that is placed in a high location, I find that using a small child tied to a long pole and holding a cup of birdseed is much safer than climbing up the ladder myself.

There is one last thing to consider when putting out a feeder and that is finding a spot where the squirrels and raccoons won't get to it. You are on your own with this one, Carl. There are a few things in life that people need to learn for themselves and this is one of them. Plus, this book is only a couple hundred pages long, which is not nearly long enough to get into the subject of both raccoon and squirrel proofing.

Now, we move on to which locations are best for birds. Try to find a spot that meets all of the above criteria and also offers some good cover and habitat. Birds need a place to get out of the wind or to hide from hawks. Many people find they have fewer birds in the winter. Some of that loss is because their feeders are too exposed. I'm sure your mother always warned you never to expose your feeder. Now you know why.

Next is a tricky one and it's not easy. Place your feeder in front of your windows where you can see it, but not where your rock-hard windows can cause damage to confused birds. Birds are often fooled by the reflections seen in windows. If bird–window collisions become a problem (and one collision is a problem), try moving your feeders just a bit. Hopefully, that will give the birds a less reflective view of your windows.

With the right choices, Carl, bird feeding can be easy for you and safe for the birds. Feeding birds should be a pleasant activity and not leave a bad taste in your mouth. Leave that job for the white chocolate.

## There's No Time to Waste When Putting Up Birdhouses

*Dear Bird Folks:*
*Over the winter my husband made several birdhouses and I can't wait to put them up. When should I put them out?*
*—Marianne,* TARRYTOWN, NY

C'mon, Marianne,

What do you mean you "can't wait to put them up?" It sounds to me like you are waiting. Put them up now. What are you waiting for, the price of rental property to go up even higher? There is no wrong time to put out birdhouses. We are not talking about tomato plants. Birdhouses can be put out any time of year, but March is probably the best time.

Birds that use nest boxes are some of our earliest nesters because unlike birds that build nests on branches of trees, they don't need to wait for the new spring foliage for protection. Also many cavity nesters (birds that use birdhouses, not birds with poor dental hygiene) are here year round. Chickadees, nuthatches, titmice, etc. are not big-time migrants, so they are closer to their breeding grounds and are ready to go earlier than those birds that need to fly up from way down south.

If you have nest boxes out in your yard from last year, you should take a few minutes to open up each one and clean it out. You'd be surprised what will move into a nest box over the winter. I've found mice living in them, sometimes wasps and bees, often piles of acorns that some mammal had stashed for the winter. Once I found a family of pygmy marmosets on vacation from Ecuador.

So, stop working on your taxes and get your nest boxes out. Just remember to keep the rent affordable or you'll end up with snobby, upscale birds that will want to put on an eighteen-room addition and turn your simple nest box into a trophy birdhouse. Then it will be only a matter of time before they post "No Trespassing" signs to keep *you* out of your own backyard.

## It's Bath Time

*Dear Bird Folks:*
*I want to get a new birdbath for my wife. Do you have*
*any suggestions?*

—*Mel,* DAYTON, OH

A question for you, Mel,

How big is your wife? She might be more comfortable in a hot tub, though that's up to you. But seriously . . .

A common mistake made by rookie birdbath buyers is getting a deep one. It seems most people like to buy deep birdbaths so they won't have to fill them as often. The birds, however, seem to like birdbaths that are fairly shallow. Try to imagine how small a finch or a chickadee is. A six-inch-deep bath is way too deep for those small birds to use, unless there is a lifeguard on duty.

Trust me, there is no advantage to a deep bath. Just because it's deep doesn't mean you don't have to clean it regularly. Remember, birds are drinking and bathing in the same water. Most people, except for my kids, would rather not do that. So it is important to keep the water fresh.

Many people seem to like painted or glazed birdbaths because they are easier to clean. However, most birds seem to like a bath that is rough or has some texture to it so they can grip it without slipping. Keep in mind most accidents happen in the bathroom; if you buy a glazed birdbath, you'd better have good insurance.

Animals love to knock over birdbaths and because of this, birdbaths tend to break. You may want to just buy a top and simply place the top on the ground. Birds are used to drinking on the ground (from puddles, ponds, etc.) and they would probably rather come to a bath that's low. Placing a bath on a pedestal is more for the esthetic benefit than for the bird's benefit. There is nothing wrong with using a pedestal, just remember to buy a few dozen extra tops.

One more thing to keep in mind is that algae will form in your birdbath during hot weather. There isn't much you can do about it, but try to scrub it out with a good stiff brush. Don't start going nuts and using all kinds of cleaners. The algae won't hurt the birds, but your cleaners might.

A quick review, Mel. When you are choosing a birdbath, pick one that is fairly shallow and has a rough texture on the inside. Remember to keep the water clean and fresh and the bath scrubbed. If that is too much work, you could always hire a pool boy to do it. I'm sure your wife wouldn't mind.

## Water and Nothing but Water

*Dear Bird Folks:*

*I saw an ad for this stuff that is supposed to keep the scum and algae out of my birdbath. Do you know anything about it? Do you think it's safe?*

—*Don*, CHARLESTON, SC

Funny you should ask, Don,

I have a customer who has been asking me the same question. She didn't like my answer, so my guess is you won't either, but here goes. No, don't put anything in your birdbath but fresh, clean water. Yeah, I know. After a few days the water looks gross and scummy. So what? Rinse it out and add more fresh water. Remember, we are talking about tap water. Unless you live in an exclusive community, where they have hot and cold running Perrier, tap water is pretty cheap. Using a stiff brush once in a while will help prevent stains from forming in your bath. But even if it does stain, relax; stains don't hurt the birds.

Algae remover, on the other hand, may not be the best to use. Would you add algae remover to your drinking water or iced tea? It may be safe or it may be unsafe, but it sure as heck isn't necessary. And it can be expensive. The company recommends adding a capful once a week, but most birdbaths are empty or need to be changed after a day or two. That's a lot of capfuls.

Forget the additives, Don. Use fresh water and a stiff brush. Then pour yourself a stiff Perrier, and both you and the birds will be better off.

## Electricity + Water . . . Sometimes They Do Mix

*Dear Bird Folks:*

*I received something called a birdbath heater for Christmas. It is a coil that I'm supposed to put in my birdbath to keep the water from freezing. The coil plugs into an electrical outlet. I was always taught that electricity and water were not a good combination. Is this product safe for me and the birds?*

—*Tom,* TRURO, MA

Hey, Tom,

When was the last time you took a shower? (And don't pretend it's the first time you've heard that question.) Or when was the last time you heated your meal of SpaghettiOs on an electric stove? Both an electric hot water heater and an electric stove use an electric coil similar to what is in your birdbath heater, except a birdbath heater won't cook SpaghettiOs. I know. I'm disappointed, too.

If you turn on an electric stove and put your hand on a burner, you won't get a shock. You'll get burned, but you won't get a shock. And, if you have an electric hot water heater, you won't get a shock when you take a shower unless you use your hair dryer at the same time. Electric heating elements, including birdbath heaters, are well insulated against any kind of moisture leakage. Still, you should connect a birdbath heater only to a grounded outlet, preferably one with a ground fault circuit interrupter (GFI). A GFI will shut off the power if there is an electrical problem and keep you from getting a shock and a permanent perm.

Be sure to use a proper outdoor extension cord and not the same extension cord you use to connect your new electric train set. Also, keep any connections off the ground. It's not cool to have the point where the two power cords meet sitting in a puddle of water. I like to wrap electrical tape around the connection of the heater and the extension cord. That helps keep out moisture and prevents the cords from coming apart when you trip over them in the dark.

Is it me or has this answer turned into a visit from Mr. Wizard? Anyhow, Tom, we sell hundreds of birdbath heaters every year and we have yet to lose one customer or bird. Go ahead and plug in your heater; it is fine to use. And if you ever figure out a way to cook SpaghettiOs in it, please let me know. I'm getting tired of eating them cold.

## Field Guides: So Many Books

*Dear Bird Folks:*

*I'm always running over to my next-door neighbor's house to ask him to identify a bird. I think he is getting a little tired of it because yesterday he said, "Why don't you buy yourself a bird book?" Hmmm, good idea. Or at least I thought it was a good idea until I went to the bookstore and became overwhelmed by all the choices. Before I invest in a new bird book, I would like to ask you which book, of all the multitudes, is the best?*

—*Jon,* BUFFALO, NY

Very wise, Jon,

You are wise to come to me before you "invest" a whopping twenty bucks in a book. Buying a book without proper counsel? Talk about living life on the edge. On the other hand, you were being very risky when you sought bird guidance from your neighbor. Neighbors are fine for borrowing things like lawn mowers or, in the case of those living in Buffalo, snow blowers. Neighbors are also good for taking in your mail while you're away. Even that can be risky depending on what magazines you subscribe to, but not as dicey as asking a neighbor for bird identification advice.

Last week, in fact, I had some guy ask me about "Beach Orioles." Beach Orioles? "What the heck are Beach Orioles?" I asked. The guy replied, "You know, the yellow orioles. My neighbor says they are Beach Orioles." I explained that the yellow birds were probably female Baltimore Orioles. I then sold the guy a new bird book and told him to stay away from his neighbor.

Even though I have a fair amount of knowledge about what birds look like, I'm constantly referring to my field guide, a.k.a. bird book. I use my field guide more than any other book, except maybe the dictionary. (Did you know that raspberry has a "p" in it? When did that happen?) The best field guides are only $20, but you would be surprised at how many people look for a cheaper way out.

The first thing they ask for is a poster. A poster? We are talking about birds, not America's most wanted. A recently published field guide of eastern birds included 650 species of birds and 4,200 illustrations. A poster large enough to include that many birds could pull your wall down, trapping your entire family. Forget the poster.

The next thing to forget is a book that tries to limit the number of birds you can see. Don't waste your time with *Birds of the Backyard* or *Fifty Easy-to-Learn Birds.* Any bonehead can learn the easy birds; it's the tough birds we need help with. The other problem is if a book only includes a few selected birds, you'll be forced to invent your own names when the bird you see isn't in there. A book that only shows the bright orange male Baltimore Oriole leaves you guessing when the dull, yellow female arrives. The resulting lack of information leads to the birth of such oddly named species as the elusive Beach Oriole.

Next on the list are the dreaded photo guides. Photo guides are exactly what the name implies: normal bird books that use photographs. Photos seem like a great idea. What can be wrong with a nice photo? The trouble is that a photo only depicts that particular bird, on that day, and in that lighting. A bird may look different depending on the weather or how the light hits its feathers. Just today a friend called me about a sleek gray bird she saw in her yard. She didn't believe me when I told her it was a catbird. The photo of the catbird in her book showed a bird that was fat and fluffy, instead of being thin and sleek like it actually is. This poor bird looked like it had gotten caught in the spin cycle of a Maytag. Don't get a photo guide, Jon.

By far, the better books are the guides that use illustrations. An artist can show the bird in several plumages and several positions, including flight. The more illustrations and the more positions, the better chance you have of making a correct identification.

There are several such field guides to consider. The three most popular are by Roger Tory Peterson, David Sibley, and *National Geographic.* All are excellent guides and it would be hard to choose the best. In fact, birders have gotten into fistfights arguing over which book is better. Ha! Birders getting into a fistfight. Can you imagine? I even made myself laugh with that one.

The one exception to this bonanza of illustrated guides is Kenn Kaufman's *Birds of North America.* He uses more than 2,000 digitally enhanced images, combined with accurate text, to help us identify each bird. Kaufman clearly labels and explains key field marks and behaviors, which assists with distinguishing even the toughest birds. This would be an excellent choice for anyone who is able to read at least a few simple words strung together.

Check out any of these guides, Jon, or any of the complete guides that contain all the birds, not just the pretty ones. However, if you find a guide that has pictures of Beach Orioles on the cover, just put it down and walk away.

## Binoculars: Try Before You Buy

*Dear Bird Folks:*
*I want to buy my dad a pair of binoculars for Father's Day but*
*I don't know anything about them. Do you have any sugges-*
*tions? I need your guidance.*

—*Sal,* OCEAN CITY, MD

Whoa, Sal,

You need *my* guidance? That's a scary thought. But I agree
with you; binoculars make a wonderful gift. A good pair of binoculars will help you see that the duck out in the ocean is really a
loon, or what appears to be a crow sitting in a tree is actually a
hawk. Binoculars also make it easy for you to check out the parties your neighbors keep "forgetting" to invite you to.

The first thing you need to decide is how much you want to
spend. For around $100, you should be able to find a pair of
binoculars that are good enough for studying the birds in your
backyard. If your dad is into nature big time, he may appreciate a
more expensive pair. However, for the sake of not filling up this
entire section with "bino" chat, I'm going to assume that an average pair of binoculars will suit his needs.

The next thing is size. With binoculars, like many things in
life, size can be an issue. To make things simple, let's just say that
binoculars come in two sizes: full-size and compact models. Most
men seem to like full-size binoculars. It's not a macho thing;
anyone, man or woman, with large hands could have trouble
comfortably working small binoculars. Compact binoculars are
wonderful, but not if you have large hands.

The next thing is magnification. Here is where macho does
become an issue. Many men think the more magnification, the
better. They think that because they are stupid. Unlike telescopes

and spotting scopes that are placed on steady tripods, binoculars are handheld. No matter how steady we think we are, we all shake a little, even if we are totally sober. If your binos are too strong, the image that you are looking at will be large but blurry.

We find that most folks can comfortably hold eight power (8x) binoculars, which bring things eight times closer. A few people can hold a ten power (10x) pair but I don't know how they do it. And no matter what you do, don't buy zoom binoculars. Zoom binoculars have a secret lever that lets you "zoom" up to 16x or more. These kinds of binoculars are basically gimmicks, have poor-quality optics, break easily, and are mostly made for people who believe infomercials.

Also, avoid perma-focus binoculars. Perma-focus binos don't have that little focusing wheel and are preset at the factory to focus on objects at an average distance. That may sound like a great idea but everyone's eyes are different and if you don't make some adjustment, you'll get eyestrain. Soon your perma-focus binoculars will give you a perma-headache. And even if you are the world's laziest slug, you still should be able to turn that little focusing wheel without totally exhausting yourself.

Find a shop that carries a large selection of binoculars. Camera stores, sporting goods stores, and, of course, birding shops are good places to start. Forget about shopping online this time. The Internet is great for finding hotels or peeking at pictures of swimsuit models, but choosing binos is a hands-on experience. Buying binoculars without trying them is like sending away for false teeth; they may not fit your face. Some kinds of binoculars work better for people with narrow faces, while other styles are best for fatheads, like fathers.

A safe choice for new binoculars for your dad, Sal, would be to spend around $100 for a full-size eight power. It should say 8 x 40 on the box (I'll explain the "40" some other day). Try to find a well-stocked shop with knowledgeable sales clerks. Look for the clerks with the best tans; at least you'll know they go outside once in a while.

## The Dull Second Number

*Dear Bird Folks:*
*You recently talked about binoculars but didn't explain the second number in a pair of 8 x 40 binoculars. Could you explain it because I've never understood it?*
—*Carl,* LOS ANGELES, CA

Okay, Carl,

I'll explain it, but it ain't gonna be pretty. Get ready to be bored.

On a pair of 8 x 40 binoculars, the second number after the power (after the "8 x") refers to the size of the objective lens (the front lens, not the eyepiece). The best way to remember which lens is which is to keep in mind that the eyepiece is the lens that goes against your eye (duh) and the objective lens is the lens that is closer to the *object* you are looking at. Unless, of course, you are holding the binoculars backward and then I don't even want to talk to you.

The bigger the number, the bigger the lens. In this case, the "40" equals 40 mm (millimeters). So, a pair of binoculars that is 8 x 40 means it has a 40 mm objective lens. An 8 x 25 pair would only have a 25 mm objective lens and thus would be a much smaller binocular.

Just about everybody in the world seems to think that the bigger the objective lens, the bigger the field of view, and the more you'll see while looking through the binoculars. But everybody in the world is wrong. The field of view is determined in the eyepiece. A large objective lens allows more light to enter your binoculars, and that's about it. Oh, two more things: Big lenses help to make the binoculars annoyingly heavy, and they are a great place to store smudges and fingerprints.

Why would anyone want a bigger objective lens? In poor light bigger binoculars will give you a brighter image, but in normal daylight they really aren't much of an advantage. Then it simply becomes a matter of which style fits comfortably in your hands.

That's enough bino talk for a while, Carl. I hope this helps and thanks for the question. However, I have the feeling that only the geeks at Cal Tech are still reading this. Everyone else has probably nodded off by now.

# 5.

## I Like Birds, but . . .

You would think that most of the questions I hear every day would be from people who are excited about seeing birds and want to know how they can see more of them. Well, think again. The vast majority of questions I receive are from people who are upset with birds for one reason or another. The birds are too noisy, too messy, too many jays, not enough cardinals, too many cardinals, not enough noisy-messy jays. Woodpeckers are forever pecking on something they shouldn't. The big birds are always "scaring away" the little birds. And don't *ever* mention squirrels in mixed company. Feeding birds is fun, but it's not a perfect pastime, and somebody is always ready to remind me of that.

## Way Too Many Grackles

*Dear Bird Folks:*

*Grackles, grackles, they raise my hackles. Can anything be done to discourage those yellow-eyed gluttons?*

—*EDK,* CAPE COD, MA

Dear Mr., Mrs., or Ms. EDK,

So the grackles raise your hackles, eh? Cute phrasing. Do you read a lot of Dr. Seuss? As usual, the reason why grackles are a problem is because people have messed things up. A couple hundred years ago, we had few, if any, grackles in this area. But then along came the Europeans with their axes and tea bags. The new farms that quickly engulfed the Northeast provided the perfect habitat for hungry grackles. Over the next few centuries, the grackle population grew to the lovable millions we have today. And you are not alone; many angry grain farmers also have grackle issues.

But before you break out the tar and feathers, or in this case just the tar, you should know that your grackles are also beneficial birds. Homeowners with their boring green lawns should love grackles because they eat tons of harmful bugs and grubs. They also eat lots of insects that attack our plants and gardens—such as June bugs and Japanese and rose beetles. And if you are thinking about pulling up your lawn and planting cotton, those piggish grackles will eat boll weevils, too.

As you have pointed out, grackles like to eat and they are omnivorous. They will eat anything they can, including the sunflower seed at our feeders. Grackles are most abundant at feeders during spring and fall migrations, but there are plenty around in the summer, too. One reason grackles are so common at feeders is that they have small territories. A male cardinal nesting in your yard may keep all the other cardinals away from your yard and feeder. But grackles will only defend a few feet around their nest. They don't care how many other grackles come to the nearest feeder. You know that house in the neighborhood where all the kids show up to eat? Well, that is what your feeder is like to the grackles. The grackles think you have the party house. When was the last time you heard that?

There are a few things you can do to help slow down those "yellow-eyed gluttons." A thistle feeder will get you lots of cutesy goldfinches and absolutely no grackles. You could also try using safflower seed in one of your feeders. Safflower is one of the grackles' least favorite foods and most of the time they will leave it alone. Safflower is not a repellent, it's just not their favorite; so if you use it, don't mix it with other seeds. And as an added bonus, squirrels and raccoons are also not big fans of safflower seed.

A few bird feeders will keep off grackles but those feeders are hard to find. Next time you are in Feeders-R-Us, or wherever you buy your feeders, look them straight in the eye and ask if they will guarantee that the feeders will keep off the grackles, because some feeders work better than others.

As you are sticking voodoo pins into your little stuffed grackle, try to keep in mind that grackles eat lots of bugs. The same bugs that we try to kill with nasty poisons, grackles will eat for free and do it safely. If all else fails, you can be sure that on Cape Cod as well as in many other northern locations, the grackles will migrate and be gone by the end of October. And that is more than I can say for your little "grackles raise my hackles" poem, which will probably be stuck in my head for the rest of the year. Thanks a lot for that.

## Pretty Blue Pigs

*Dear Bird Folks:*

*What is going on with the Blue Jays? I haven't seen much of them for the past few months and now they are hitting my feeder from all directions. Where have they been and why are they suddenly so hungry?*

—*Mandy,* CHATHAM, MA

Oh, Mandy,

Aren't Blue Jays the best? They are so handsome and rowdy. To me they always look like they are ready for a party or a fight, or both. It is odd that a bird that has such presence will seemingly disappear, be almost forgotten, and then explode back on the scene almost instantly. Where do they go? They have been right in your neighborhood all along. They never leave, but they do get quiet. During the summer nesting season, they are off being good parents and like all parents, there is very little partying for them while they raise the kids. Fortunately for Blue Jays, their kids are raised and on their own in a matter of months, and then it's back to party time.

Fall is when Blue Jays get back together in small flocks and look for food. Jays are one of the few birds that gather and store food. When they find a source of food, they load up by holding as much as they can carry in their throats. Jays don't have real crops like chickens, but their throats are able to stretch a bit and that allows them to jam in a few extra sunflower seeds before they fly off.

They might fly away to eat the seeds, but often in the fall they stash the seeds in a tree cavity or bury them in the ground. The hidden seeds are sometimes eaten later when food is scarce, but many times they can't remember where they have hidden the food (probably the result of too much partying). The undiscovered seeds and acorns then sprout into trees or other plants, thus making Blue Jays responsible for growing at least some of their own food.

Eventually, the fall gathering of food will slow down and the Blue Jays won't be such pigs. As winter sets in, the Blue Jay flocks break up and they will come less regularly to your feeder. Your feeder will then be attended by a more deserving visitor, like the gray squirrel.

## Protecting Feeders from Squirrels (Good Luck!)

*Dear Bird Folks:*

*I just received a bird feeder as a gift. I have never fed the birds before and have been warned that I need to put some protection around my feeder or my new gift will be nothing but a feeder for squirrels. Does my new feeder need protection and if so, what is the best way to protect it?*

—*Jim,* KNOXVILLE, TN

Oh no, Jim,

For years I have avoided answering questions about squirrel-proofing bird feeders. Why? First, most questions written to us about squirrels are filled with so many nasty words that even the *New York Post* wouldn't print them. Second, and most importantly, I know what is going to happen the minute I offer squirrel-proofing advice. I will be hit with a wave of bitter calls, letters, e-mails, and notes tied to rocks and thrown through the front window from people who didn't have perfect results from some of my suggestions.

And that's not the worst of it. I routinely get accosted at work or in the aisles of Stop & Shop by people with photos. That's right, photos! Some people seem to derive great pleasure from showing me pictures of a squirrel at their feeder. It's as if I wouldn't believe them without some kind of illustration. Anyhow, I'll try to help you out here, Jim, but remember these are only suggestions. If they work for you, great. But if they don't work, I don't want to see the photos, hear from your lawyer, or wake up with a horse's head at the foot of my bed.

There is no way you can overestimate the cleverness of the Eastern Gray Squirrel. They can do it all: climb, jump, swim (bet you didn't know that), dig, chew, and according to some, spit acid and breathe fire (you probably knew that). They have the jumping skills of a kangaroo, the grabbing ability of a spider monkey, and the brains of a chess champion. And it all comes in a twenty-four-ounce package.

Every day, people tell me they have had a great squirrel-proof feeder for years and suddenly the squirrels are beating it. Why? Because they are the only creatures that appear to evolve in their own lifetime. Most life forms take millions of years to evolve subtle changes; squirrels can evolve overnight. If they can't reach a feeder one day, they will wake up the next day with a newly grown five-foot-long arm. Or so it would seem.

When dealing with squirrels it is important to have the right attitude. If you are someone who looks at life as an adventure, you'll be fine. But if you are the type of person who is stubborn and easily gets upset when things don't go as planned, you are a dead man. The squirrels will own you and every waking minute of your day. You'll be banging on the windows, running through the backyard screaming at them, and be a total embarrassment to your entire family. And you won't care.

Yes, to answer your question, Jim, you will definitely need protection. When it comes to bird feeding and a few other things in life, always use protection. Since I don't know exactly what your feeder looks like, I simply suggest you place it on a metal pole.

Pole-mounted feeders are the easiest to squirrel-proof, if you keep a few things in mind.

First, you must place the pole out in the open. By "in the open," I mean away from trees, fences, porches, speeding trains, or anything else a squirrel can leap from. Ten feet away is the rule of thumb, but it is only a rule of thumb. It is not an exact law of physics. Sometimes six or eight feet is enough and other times two hundred feet won't work. In addition, the pole should be about six feet tall. Squirrels can easily jump five feet straight up from the ground, and that's on a bad day.

Next, you will need a squirrel baffle for your pole. (Yes, squirrels can climb metal poles.) Invest in a real baffle, made by a real company and sold by a real store that knows about such things. Don't waste your time greasing the pole or using an old coffee can or an upside-down salad bowl as a baffle. For the most part, none of that homemade stuff works. It only helps raise your blood pressure and lower your property value.

Good luck with your new feeder, Jim. Try not to get too upset with squirrels, though. Remember, we do this for a hobby; they do it for a living.

## Sleep Late . . . Some Birds Will Still Be Singing

*Dear Bird Folks:*

*I have two questions. I woke up at 4:30 the other morning to a wall of bird songs. Birds were singing everywhere. I looked out the window but didn't see a single bird. A few hours later, at the more normal time of 7 A.M., there were almost no birds singing. Why were the birds singing so early and why couldn't I see them? Also, what is the best way to learn birdcalls?*

—*Phyllis,* EVANSVILLE, IN

First, Phyl,

With no offense to the Evansville school system, I might suggest that you take a quick refresher course in mathematics. Right at the top, you said you had "two questions," when you clearly have asked three. Go ahead; take a quick count. There are three questions, aren't there? Are you a bit tired? What happened? Did you get up too early this morning, say, around 4:30? Don't worry. I can probably answer all three questions at no extra charge. Just don't tell the union.

As most people already know, even the ones in Evansville, birds don't typically sing for fun or entertainment; they sing to communicate. What you may not know is that, with few exceptions, the males do all the singing. They sing to attract a mate and to announce their territory. Each day, as soon as possible, the males want to make sure that everyone knows they are alive and well and ready to defend their territory. Although it may all sound the same to us, there is some evidence suggesting that each bird has its own unique song and other birds know it. We may hear the lovely call of a robin, while other robins hear, "Hey, this is Vinny. Stay away and nobody gets hurt."

Another reason why birds sing at the crack of dawn is that the predawn hours are usually the quietest part of the day. The sun hasn't had a chance to stir up the air. The birds' voices are a lot clearer without having to compete with the sound of the wind blowing through trees or having to be heard above those annoying backup beeps on dump trucks.

The reason you can't see the birds, Phyl, is because they have just gotten up and most of them are probably still singing in the shower. Also, early morning light is poor and summer foliage is thick. Even brightly colored birds like cardinals can be tough to find if they don't want to be seen.

Which brings us to the last in your string of questions. What is the best way to learn birdcalls? Well, you don't want to start at 4:30 A.M. As we said, the light is bad, plus there are way too many birds singing at once. You'll be overwhelmed. In addition, who needs the hassle of explaining to the cops why you are walking through your neighborhood with binoculars at 4:30 in the morning? As you've noticed, there are fewer birds singing at 7 A.M. I would go out then, when there are fewer choices, the light is better, and the neighbors are less paranoid.

For me, the absolute best way to learn a birdcall is to choose a call you don't know and track the bird down and don't give up until you find it. The harder the bird is to find, the more likely you are to remember its song. Once you find the bird, listen carefully to its song and try to come up with your own catchphrase or rhyme to help you remember. There are tapes and CDs that are helpful too, but nothing is better or more rewarding than finding the bird and seeing it while it sings.

The last way to identify a birdcall is to phone me and sing the call. I may not be able to identify it, but at least I'll be entertained for a few minutes. And I promise I won't put you on speakerphone. Not!

## Woodpeckers Don't Always Peck Wood

*Dear Bird Folks:*
*Every year at this time I'm visited by a male flicker that hammers*
*at my metal chimney cap. Is he doing this to attract a mate or is*
*he announcing his territory? Whatever it is, just don't tell me*
*that he is hacking at my steel cap to correct an iron deficiency.*
— *Marjorie,* YARMOUTH PORT, MA

Good one, Marjorie,
Iron deficiency. Ha! I like that. I might use that line someday.
If I do, I'll send you a quarter.

Spring is the season that woodpeckers, like most birds
and other living things, respond to the most. And flickers, as most
of you know, are woodpeckers . . . big woodpeckers. They are
second only to the behemoth Pileated Woodpecker, our largest woodpecker.

You were right on both counts when you asked if the flicker
was trying to attract a mate or announcing its territory, but there
is more to it than that. It is thought that flickers mate for life, but
not in the sense that the pair is together 24/7. It's more a case of
convenience, since they both return to the same breeding location each year. When the male bird returns from down south, he
is likely to find the same female has also returned. The flicker
that was drumming on your chimney is simply saying, "Honey, I'm
home," but without offering any explanation about what he has
been up to all winter.

Although they have a call, woodpeckers don't have a true
song, which is why they use loud drumming to announce their
presence. Hollow trees work fine as sounding boards but hollow
metal gutters or chimney caps work even better. Years ago, I
remember being woken up at dawn by a sound I thought was the

telephone, only to discover that it was a flicker drumming on my neighbor's aluminum boat. Most people would have been annoyed but I thought it was pretty funny, though not nearly as funny as the sight of me racing through the house in my underwear, trying to answer a phone call from a mating flicker.

Flickers are fairly large birds, but their carpentry skills aren't the best so they look for soft wood to drill. A rotting dead tree is a dream location to a flicker although our fixation with parklike property has made dead trees hard to find. The birds hate to give them up and return to them each year. I'm sure if you look around, Marjorie, you'll find a fabulously rotting tree surviving somewhere in your neighborhood. If you check it out, there is a good chance you'll find your flickers nesting in it.

What about stopping woodpeckers from drumming? I know you didn't specifically ask about this, but you are just about the only one who hasn't lately. This time of year, twelve out of every ten questions I get are about how to stop woodpeckers from drumming on buildings. Harmless drumming on metal is exactly that, harmless; however, woodpeckers drilling on wooden shingles can cause serious damage. Stopping them from drilling holes into your house isn't easy. I have yet to find a surefire solution, but here are a few ideas that have worked at least for some people in the past. You may want to remember some of these in case things turn ugly with your flicker.

Since woodpeckers are territorial, putting up mirrors may be effective. The bird won't be able to drive off its own image and it may move on. Hanging those flashy Mylar strips has also worked for some, as well as the plastic owls and fake rubber snakes. The rubber snake worked great for me until a raccoon chewed off its head.

Whatever you do, it's important to remember that it has to happen at the exact point of contact, which is usually some impossible-to-reach location on your house. A fake snake on your back porch won't do much good when the birds are drilling on the third floor roof peak.

The other thing to remember is that you don't need to "get rid" of your woodpecker but simply to discourage it from eating your house. Woodpeckers aren't evil, and they are interesting birds to watch. Although I must admit they would be even more interesting to watch if they were banging on the neighbor's house.

## Fighting Female Hummingbirds . . . Not Only on Cable TV

*Dear Bird Folks:*
*After trying all summer, I have finally attracted some humming-*
*birds to my feeder. However, I only have dull birds that look like*
*females and all they do is fight each other. How can I stop the*
*fighting and how can I get some pretty male hummingbirds to*
*visit my feeders?*

—*Molly,* ANNANDALE-ON-HUDSON, NY

Really, Molly?
Is there really a town called "Annandale-on-Hudson?" That's
not a town, it's a sentence. You should be glad Annandale isn't on
Lake Winnipesauke in New Hampshire. You'd have to buy extra
long envelopes just to fit your return address.

118

As for your fighting hummers, don't worry about it. Hummingbirds love to fight each other. That's what they live for. Hummingbirds are so small that almost every creature on earth can beat them up. Fish, frogs, spiders, dragonflies, and praying mantises have all made a meal out of hummingbirds. In order to push something around, they pick on each other.

Most birds only defend a breeding territory but hummingbirds are one of the few birds that will defend a food source. Almost anywhere a hummer finds food it is ready to fight to defend it, even along its migration route to Central America. However, since it only weighs a zillionth of an ounce, the only thing it can attack, without being laughed at, is another hummingbird and the occasional ladybug.

What to do about the fighting birds at your feeder? You could try talking to them and perhaps suggest some anger management classes. Or you could put out another feeder or two. Hang your second feeder in another part of your yard, out of sight from your first feeder. That way one hummer can't control both feeders. Putting out two feeders not only controls some of the fighting, it also helps me sell more hummingbird feeders, and I like that.

You may only have females at your feeder, but you may also have some young males mixed in. They look very similar. The reason you don't have any adult males is that most of them have headed out already. Male hummingbirds aren't very good parents and as soon as the kids start yelling, they are outta there. The females stay a few weeks longer to raise the kids and to show them how to find food.

Good luck with your hummingbirds, Molly. Thanks for the question and I hope to see you the next time you visit Cape-Cod-on-Atlantic.

## Dropping Droppings into the Birdbath

*Dear Bird Folks:*
*For some strange reason, the grackles in my area have been flying*
*over my birdbath and attacking it with their droppings. The*
*grackles seem to go out of their way to dump their waste into my*
*birdbath. My friend says they do the same thing to her swimming*
*pool. Why do grackles keep dropping their droppings into water?*
— *Marcy,* MARSTONS MILLS, MA

Why, Marcy?

Why do grackles keep dropping their droppings into water? Doesn't everybody? That does not sound odd to me. That's what the generous people of Boston do, only they call it the Outfall Pipe, so they can share their droppings with their coastal neighbors.

You might be surprised to hear this, but we get a lot of questions about grackle bombing attacks. Pools, tennis courts, and big cars appear to be their favorite targets. It seems that the grackles have the same issues with opulence that many of us do. However, while most of us just complain about rich people, the grackles actually do something about it. And yes, the grackles are going out of their way to attack your friend's pool.

Here is the unusual part: The grackles aren't hitting your birdbath with their own droppings. As strange as it may sound, they are most likely dropping another bird's poop into your bath. You are now thinking that the summer heat and traffic have finally gotten to me, but it is true.

The gross stuff in your birdbath may not belong to the bird that dropped it. How is that possible, you ask? It's a housekeeping thing. In order to keep their nests clean, most baby songbirds give off their waste in what is called a "fecal sack." These little pouches of poop are mostly white and are encased in a tough mucous membrane. After being fed, the baby bird will turn its back to the parent and "hand" it this sack. The parent bird will then fly away with the sack and drop it a short distance away from the nest. (And I thought dealing with diapers was gross.)

If you think that is disgusting, this next bit of information will really curl your toes. Instead of flying away with the waste, many birds, including bluebirds, will often eat the fecal sacks. There's a pleasant thought. Perhaps that explains why bluebirds always carry a pack of Tic-Tacs.

Most birds drop these sacks randomly as they fly, but often grackles will target a specific dumping ground. One theory is that hundreds of years ago, before so much land was cleared, grackles nested along the edges of lakes and rivers. Grackles, which often nest in colonies, wanted to hide their nesting sites from predators, so they would drop fecal sacks in the nearby water. Perhaps the attacks on our birdbaths and pools are a remnant of this behavior. Green tennis courts could indeed fool the birds into thinking they are small, algae-filled ponds. However, I'm convinced that their attacks on big, fancy cars are done purely for fun, and who can blame them for that?

Grackles are birds many people love to hate. But like so many things we complain about, we only have ourselves to blame. The rather large grackle population is a direct result of settlers clearing land and creating the perfect grackle nesting habitat.

The good news, Marcy, is that soon the nesting season will be over and these bombing attacks on your birdbath and your friend's pool should stop. In the meantime, just keep cleaning out your birdbath water. And when you visit your friend's pool, wear a plastic hat.

## Birdseed and Bugs, All in the Same Package (and No Extra Charge)

*Dear Bird Folks:*
*Thanks to my bag of birdseed, I now have a house full of moths.*
*The moths are everywhere and my seed is full of webs and worms.*
*Where did these moths come from, why are they in my seed, and*
*how can I get rid of them?*

*—Paul,* BEVERLY, MA

First, Paul,

Let me tell you a story. Thirty years ago, when I first started feeding birds, I bought a fifty-pound bag of sunflower seed at the end of winter. In those days, bird feeding was still based on old wives' tales and voodoo. Just about everybody took down their feeders when the snow melted. Not wanting to violate the unwritten bird feeding code, I too put my feeders away for the summer. Thinking I was ahead of the game for the next feeding season, I smugly put my fifty-pound bag of seed in my attic, where it would stay nice and dry until fall.

One hot August day, I went into the attic for some reason, probably to put away the last of the Christmas ornaments. When I opened the door to the attic, it actually looked like Christmas, a white Christmas. Millions of moths were flying about like winged snowflakes. And they were all coming from that bag of seed I had shrewdly bought on sale. I'm sure you are wondering by now what I did about it. What do you think I did? I sold the house and moved out of town.

Let me explain a little about these moths. We are talking about "meal moths," which are moths that seem to enjoy our food as much as we do. They eat grains, crackers, cereal, and in your case, birdseed. They are not the same moths that eat cloth, so your silk underwear is totally safe. Actually, the moths don't eat anything; it is those little nasty worms (the larvae) that do all the eating. The moths are just flying around looking for unprotected food to lay eggs in.

How did you end up with these lovely moths, you ask? Well, they can be carried into your house in just about any food, especially untreated foods like health food or pet foods. In your case (and mine), the pet food was birdseed.

What to do about it? Prevention is important. (I know that for you, Paul, it's too late for prevention, but I have to assume that you are not the only person reading this.) Use up your seed quickly. It takes at least thirty days for meal moths to go through their life cycle and much longer if kept cool. In the summer, buy smaller amounts of seed. Never store birdseed in your house. Heat from your house will cause the eggs to hatch and grow quickly. A shed or garage is the best place to store your seeds. The moths will still hatch out in the shed but who cares? It's a shed.

Getting rid of the moths is tough. You will need to put all your grains, cereals, pastas, etc. into airtight containers. Inspect any opened packages for webs, the telltale sign of the larvae. Some garden centers sell moth traps that work well. The traps have no pesticides; they use a pheromone sex scent as bait that is great at attracting moths and the occasional swinger.

You are not alone here, Paul. It seems that I write about this every year. Meal moths are a big problem, especially for those of us who sell seed. The hot weather makes them hatch out and there isn't much we can do about it. Storing seed outside your house and buying a smaller amount in the summer is about the best you can do.

You could also do what I did: sell your house and move out of town. But you may find that putting out a few moth traps is the less expensive option.

## The Birds Won't Complain about Your Dirty Windows

*Dear Bird Folks:*
*Yet another gorgeous cardinal lies dead on my patio, the second*
*one this year, plus a Blue Jay and a Downy Woodpecker. Our*
*patio is surrounded by five large sliding glass doors. Evidently,*
*the birds are seeing their reflections at certain times of the day.*
*Please advise me how to keep from killing more birds. I love the*
*birds but I feel like a murderer.*

—*Alice,* BASS RIVER, MA

Calm down, Alice,

You are not a murderer. Well, not in this case. I don't know your history or what else you have been up to, but my guess is that anyone concerned about a cardinal's welfare does not have any homicides on her record . . . or at least very few.

What you have described is one of the biggest problems facing birds throughout the developed world. Think about this: If four birds died from just your one house, there could very well be four dead birds for every building in the United States. That would equal, um, well, a lot of dead birds and maybe more. It is estimated that in this country alone, close to 950 million birds die from window collisions each year. Without a doubt, window strikes are one of the greatest contributors to bird deaths. They are right up there with deaths caused by outdoor cats, habitat destruction, and eating undercooked worms.

You were right, Alice, when you mentioned reflections being the cause, but it is not the birds seeing their own reflections that is the problem, as it is when territorial birds attack the windows. It is the reflection of the trees and the sky that causes the trouble. Your window acts as a mirror and the birds mistakenly think they can fly to a tree, which is actually an image on a hard pane of glass.

Since the victim birds you have described are all feeder birds, it is pretty safe to assume that you have bird feeders. As strange as it may seem, the best way to protect feeder birds is to move your feeders closer to your windows. When feeders are only two or three feet from a window, the feeding birds are well aware of its presence. Even if a bird doesn't realize the window is there because it happens to be severely nearsighted or just daft, the closeness of the window prevents the bird from flying into it with enough speed to do serious harm. Feeders that are fifteen or twenty feet from a window often cause the most problems.

In addition to moving your feeders closer to the house, several items can be applied to your windows that will help break up the reflections and alert the birds to the danger. Before I get into it, it should be noted that any item you use to break up reflections must go outside the window. The problematic reflections also prevent birds from seeing inside.

Decals of hawk silhouettes have been used for years but recent studies question their effectiveness. Also, many people who live in glass houses hate to spoil their million-dollar view by putting black decals on their windows. So, an "invisible" decal was developed. Birds have the ability to see ultraviolet while us human dullards cannot. Some company developed a decal that looks nearly invisible to us, but the birds are able to see it just fine.

Another new item is a bit more annoying to look at but is probably the most effective. About ten years ago, a woman told me that she virtually stopped all bird–window collisions by taping streamers of short ribbons to her windows. The flapping motion alerted the birds. A decade later, some company is selling a similar item that appears to be doing the job. The device is called Feather Guard. The package contains lengths of fishing line with colored feathers tied to them, which attach to the window with suction cups. The idea is that the loose feathers naturally catch a bird's attention. Early reports are that this new product is indeed saving birds, plus it gives your house that year-round Mardi Gras look.

Over the years I have tried several items on my own windows, but I find that the lazy method works the best. I simply never wash my windows. After a while the built-up dirt and grime not only prevents the deadly reflections, but it gives me shade in the summer and adds a much needed layer of insulation in the winter. Once again laziness pays off, which is really lucky for me.

# 6.

## Mystery Birds Identified and Explained

The thing most birders hate is when someone walks up to them on the street, or at a party, or when they are being prepped for surgery and says, "I saw an unusual bird the other day . . ." After that statement comes a long, vague, and often contradictory description of a bird they caught a glimpse of while doing seventy-five on the interstate. Birders hate it because in most instances they can't ID the bird from the description, which is embarrassing for them because the only thing birders know about is birds. Even if they are able to identify the bird, the person asking isn't going to be happy unless the bird they saw is rare and there is some kind of monetary reward for seeing one. The nice thing about writing a response to the "what bird did I see?" question is that I can't see the hurt look in the person's eyes when the wonderful mystery bird turns out to be the ubiquitous House Finch. Even if the bird was a big owl or a handsome bunting, I usually say that it was a House Finch. It's so much easier that way. For me, anyhow.

## A Bird with Horns

*Dear Bird Folks:*

*Don't make fun of me, but I think I have a new kind of finch in my yard. This odd bird looks and acts very much like a female House Finch, but it has those horns on the top of its head. I swear I'm not making this up. I can't find it in my bird book. Is there such a bird as a Horned House Finch?*

*—Terry,* W. HARWICH, MA

Make fun of you, Terry?

Why would I make fun of you? I never make fun of anybody, do I? Just because you have a bird with horns on its head flying around your yard isn't any reason for me to make fun of you. Besides, if I make you angry, you might send your Devil Finch to poke me with its pitchfork.

Let's see, a horned bird in August, eh? That's odd. If it were May I would understand; there are lots of horny birds around in the springtime. By late summer the nesting season is all but over and our yards are filled with goofy-looking juvenile birds. The horned birds you are seeing are nothing more than brand-new finches that haven't totally lost their baby down yet. We see these freaky finches every year. Occasionally, some young birds keep a few tufts of feathers on the top of their heads even after their juvenile feathers have grown in, giving them a horned look. In a few weeks, the molt will be complete and the horns will be gone. You'll be safe from the flying devil's pitchfork attacks for another year or at least until Halloween.

You shouldn't feel too badly about being fooled by the horned finches, Terry. Lots of people have been calling about them. Late summer is probably the toughest time of year to identify birds. We hear from more bewildered people in August than any other time of year, not counting Election Day.

Why are birds so tough to ID right now? As I've already pointed out, we are suddenly up to our necks in baby birds. Some baby birds look just like their parents, while others look like they were adopted from overseas. Birds such as chickadees, which are the world's best birds, don't create any confusion at all. They look like the adults the minute they step out of the nest. Chickadees are way too cool to ever have an immature look. But then there are the young robins that don't look anything like the adults. Instead of having the slate-gray back and signature brick-red breast, the young robins are all washed out and speckled. They'll remind you more of the acne-faced teenager working the drive-thru at Burger Land than a classic robin.

Besides robins, birds such as bluebirds, waxwings, cardinals, tanagers, and orioles are among the species of songbirds that spend the first few months of their life dressed differently than their parents. I guess the same thing could be said about humans. My kids don't dress like I do, which is just as well. I wouldn't want them borrowing one of my leisure suits.

## It's a Bluebird . . . or a Grosbeak . . . or a Bunting

*Dear Bird Folks:*
*Last week I had this different bird under my feeder. It was solid blue, about the size of a chickadee. My bird book suggests that it was an Eastern Bluebird, a Blue Grosbeak or an Indigo Bunting. Do you have any suggestions as to which it was and will it stay in my yard all summer?*

—*Brenda,* HYANNIS, MA

Cool, Brenda,

A multiple-choice quiz! First, let me get a No. 2 pencil, clear the books off my desk, put my feet flat on the floor, and keep my eyes forward. Now, what was your question again? Oh yeah, something about an all-blue bird. Let's see, your mystery bird couldn't be either an Eastern Bluebird or a Blue Grosbeak because, in spite of their names, neither of those birds is all blue. According to your clue, the mystery bird was "solid blue." Plus, both of those birds are larger than a chickadee. That leaves us with a clear winner. The answer to your question is: c) Indigo Bunting. But here is the odd part: The bird that you saw, the Indigo Bunting, isn't blue at all or even indigo, it is black. Calm down, I'll explain in a minute.

Here on Cape Cod, Indigo Buntings are a springtime treat. In April and May, we get lots of calls from lucky people who find blue-looking mystery birds under their feeders. The curious thing is that just about everywhere else, Indigo Buntings are common. Nobody gets excited about them but us. Their summer range runs from the East Coast, west to Texas and all those rectangle-shaped states. Even the rest of Massachusetts has plenty of them. They are common throughout our entire state, except for the Cape. Buntings apparently can't handle all the tourists.

Like many spring birds, Indigo Buntings spend the winter way down in the tropics and need to make the long migration north to their breeding grounds. It is thought that strong winds sometimes force migrating birds to fly over the ocean. (Pay attention here, Brenda, this is important.) The migrating buntings, which are trying to get to anyplace *but* Cape Cod, are forced by the winds to land here. These tired and hungry birds chow at our feeders, which is interesting since feeder visits aren't all that common once nesting begins. Then, after a quick stop for refueling, the buntings move on.

The breeding plumage of the male Indigo Bunting is the striking solid blue that everyone gets excited about. The female bunting, on the other hand, is a drab, generic brown and often goes unnoticed. I'll bet most people pass the female off as some kind of sparrow, but this bird is dull even for a sparrow.

The male bunting is a typical pretty-boy male. When it comes to the domestic chores (you're not going to like this, Brenda), he is basically old school. He does none of the nest building, nor does he help incubate the eggs or feed the baby birds. He just sits high upon an exposed branch, looking studly, while the female does all of the "woman's work" (his words, not mine). However, once the young birds have fledged, he does take over the feeding chores and finally becomes a good father. But that is only so the female can get started on a second brood.

Now to expound on a subject that I touched upon earlier: The Indigo Bunting is not blue but black, black as coal. How can this be, when your eyes are clearly seeing that the bird is blue? The red on a cardinal, for example, is from the red pigment in the feathers. But there is no blue pigment in the bunting's feathers; the blue we see is the result of feather structure. The feathers are formed in such a way that the reflecting light makes them appear blue. When the sun shines down on the bird, it looks very blue; but if the sunlight is coming from behind, the bird looks black.

Confused, Brenda? I know, I don't get it either, but I'm just telling you what the books say.

## Nuthatches vs. Creepers

*Dear Bird Folks:*
*I have the cutest little bird coming to my yard. It acts just like a nuthatch, climbing on the trunks of my trees. But it isn't black and white like a nuthatch, and is mostly dull brown. Could it be a young nuthatch?*

—*Janet,* EASTHAM, MA

No, Janet,
Your cute little bird is not a nuthatch, young or old. The bird you describe is a Brown Creeper. That's right. The bird's real name is "Brown Creeper." The name says it all. The Brown Creeper is indeed brown and spends most of its time creeping on the trunks of trees. It is a bird with a true descriptive name, unlike the nuthatch. I've yet to figure out what that name means.

The Brown Creeper is a small, shy bird that looks more like a dried leaf than a bird. And it is more common than most of us think. Creepers are like people who drive Plymouths; they are all around us, but we rarely notice them. Creepers are rather quiet birds and have a foraging behavior that is a little different from nuthatches. The talkative nuthatch will descend the trunk of a tree headfirst while it searches for food. The creeper, on the other hand, never climbs down a tree. It always "creeps up" the trunk of the tree. If the creeper misses something, it will fly down to the base of the tree and work its way back up. It will never turn around, go back, or ask directions. You know, like when your husband is driving.

The creeper will sometimes visit our suet feeders, but it rarely stays to feed for long. It seems to be embarrassed to be taking food without a proper invitation. After a bite or two, it quickly moves on. When foraging, creepers use their long, down-curved beaks to search tree bark for insects, spider eggs, or loose change.

Brown creepers can be found throughout most of the United States but most people never take the time to notice them. What creepers need to do is hire a better publicist. Puffins, for example, are seldom seen and yet everyone knows who they are and what they look like. Stores are filled with puffin knickknacks and T-shirts but people rarely ask for a creeper knickknack. And when was the last time you saw a Brown Creeper T-shirt? A Brown Creeper T-shirt would look more like a shirt with a faded chocolate stain on it than a cool bird.

But there are advantages to being dull. The colorful puffin has to nest underground on small, isolated islands. The demure creeper can nest right under our noses (perhaps not under everyone's nose, but I know a few noses that would support a whole family of creepers). While most birds need to seek out dense foliage for protection while they sleep, the cryptic creepers can roost out in the open, clinging to the trunk of the nearest tree. There used to be a creeper that would spend the night clinging to the side of my brown-stained garage. It blended in so well that no one ever noticed it. No one noticed it but me, with my keen eye. Well, actually my eye wasn't that keen. A friend had to point the bird out to me, but you don't need to know that.

Good for you for noticing that little creeper, Janet. They are fun birds to watch, even though they are a bit dull. But there is nothing wrong with being dull. Just ask my accountant.

## Purple vs. House Finches

*Dear Bird Folks:*

*For three years in a row Purple Finches have nested in the alcove between our house and garage. We have a shelf over the door going into the garage with four pretty birdhouses on it. In the past two years, the finches have built their nest on the shelf between two of the houses. This year, they have built in the old Christmas wreath. Do Purple Finches normally nest so close to human activity?*

—*Roland,* CHATHAM, MA

You'll understand, Roland,

Because you are from Chatham. You know when some guy from out of town pronounces the name of your town *Chat-ham* instead of *Chat-em?* And you have to decide whether to say, "Dude, it is totally not pronounced *Chat-ham,*" or let it go and leave the correcting job to someone else? Well, I'm the correcting guy and my job is to point out that your Purple Finches are actually House Finches. Whether you live in Chat-ham or Chat-em, those cute little birds nesting in your alcove are House Finches.

How do I know for sure your birds are House Finches? As their first name, "house," suggests, these birds like to live around our homes. To answer your question, no, Purple Finches do not normally nest near human activity. Purple Finches like to nest alone, high up in conifers. They aren't squatters like House Finches, which love to live near us.

Purple Finches are handsome songbirds that may be found throughout much of North America but, unfortunately for you, Roland, rarely on Cape Cod. Conversely, the House Finch population is huge. They are everywhere. They are nearly as common as SUVs at a gas station. And believe it or not, House Finches are new to this area. They were introduced about sixty years ago and the population has exploded during the past few decades, while at the same time, the Purple Finch population has declined.

The knee-jerk reaction is that the newer, aggressive House Finch must be causing the decline of the Purple Finch. That may be true but no one knows for sure. The Purple Finch population decline began long before House Finches arrived in this area, so their drop-off is most likely tied to changes in habitat, rather than the arrival of another species.

The reason why many people mistakenly call the common House Finch "Purple Finch" can be blamed on the old bird books. Since the House Finch is new around here, really old field guides don't even have them pictured. The other problem is that the two species look very similar and could easily be confused with one another.

How do you tell them apart, you ask? Well, around here it's easy. Since Purple Finches are rare on the Cape, if you see more than one it will be a House Finch. And just on the odd chance that you travel off-Cape someday, I'll give you some visual clues to distinguish the two birds.

Neither bird is purple or looks like a house. The male House Finch has bright red on the head, chest, and base of the tail; the rest of the bird is sparrow brown. The male Purple Finch is a deeper red and the deep red is washed over most of the bird, including its back. The back is always brown on a House Finch, and red on the Purple Finch. Both birds have white on the belly (near the legs), but the House Finch also has brown streaking on the belly while once again, the Purple Finch has red streaking. The females have no red at all. The female Purple Finch is mostly brown with a bold stripe above the eye, while the female House Finch is basically streaky brown with nothing else worth talking about.

I mentioned that House Finches love to build in or around our buildings. As you found out, Roland, they'll build in old

Christmas wreaths or on porch lights. Their all-time favorite nesting site seems to be in hanging plants. All day long I listen to people complaining about finches nesting in their hanging plants. They want to buy a $20 birdhouse to keep the finches from nesting in their $5 hanging plant. What? Hello, McFly, just go buy a new plant and save yourself fifteen bucks. And I wonder why I don't have many friends.

## Aflac: Duck vs. Goose

*Dear Bird Folks:*
*This is a weird question, but my husband and I are having an argument. He says the white bird in the Aflac insurance television commercial is a duck and I say it's a goose. Who is right?*
—*Linda,* EASTHAM, MA

It's okay, Linda,

We live for weird questions so don't worry about that. However, I do think you and your hubby are having a little too much TV time. Since your marriage is riding on my answer, I decided to personally contact Aflac to find out for sure. It turns out that it's not a duck or a goose, but a raccoon wearing lots of makeup. Ever since they made such a mess while filming that Alfred Hitchcock movie, birds have been banned from joining the Screen Actors Guild. So, Aflac decided to offer the role to a young struggling raccoon just out of Juilliard. Wow, talk about uncovering a Hollywood secret.

It's a duck, Linda, a white domestic duck. The same kind of duck that barbaric people, like my wife, eat. A domestic goose would be about three times bigger and a lot crabbier. Sorry, I couldn't back you up, kid, but your husband was right this time. But you knew he was bound to get something right eventually.

## Hairy vs. Downy Woodpeckers

*Dear Bird Folks:*
*I have a wonderful black and white woodpecker coming to my suet feeder. My bird book shows two different woodpeckers that both look like my woodpecker. One is called a Downy Woodpecker and the other is a Hairy Woodpecker. How can I tell which one is in my yard?*

—*Rusty*, DALTON, GA

First of all, Rusty,

I'm not going to lower my incredibly high standards and make a cheap joke about whether size matters. Okay, maybe I will because in this case it does matter. The Hairy Woodpecker is much larger than the little Downy. The Hairy is typically just over nine inches tall, while the Downy is just over six inches, and he's okay with it. The problem is, however, unless you see the two birds together or like to carry a yardstick, the size reference isn't all that obvious. If it was easy, you wouldn't have had to write your note and I could be eating a dish of ice cream instead of writing this answer.

When they aren't together, identifying a Downy or a Hairy Woodpecker is like trying to recognize a politician from a regular crook. We get fooled time and time again. The best field mark for figuring out the two woodpeckers is bill length. On a Downy, the bill is about half the size of its head; on a Hairy, the bill is as large as or larger than the head. Assuming a woodpecker's head is an inch long, a Downy's bill would be about half an inch long and a Hairy's bill would be at least an inch long. Bill length is important since we don't often see the Hairy and Downy traveling together. Yet, rarely does a woodpecker go anywhere without bringing along both its own bill and head.

One other important field mark is the outside edge of the tail. A Hairy's tail is totally white, but the outer edge of a Downy's tail is white with a few black spots. The sexes of either bird are alike, except that the males have a bright red spot on the back of their heads. Some females have bright red lipstick, but those birds are usually from the city.

Sometimes behavior can tip you off. The Hairy Woodpecker is more likely to be found on a tree, while the Downy, with its smaller size, may also be found on reeds, cattails, and plant stalks. Either bird will occasionally do damage to buildings and houses, but the Downy will be the one most likely to attack your house if it's made out of cattails.

Here is something else worth knowing. The names "hairy" and "downy" refer to the clump of feathers at the base of each bird's bill. Many woodpeckers have a bushy growth of feathers at the base of their bills. This fluff is much like those silly goatees that pseudo macho men grow on their faces. The woodpecker's feathery goatee is not there to look tough or trendy, but to protect its nostrils from wood chips and dust. When a woodpecker digs out a cavity in a tree, small bits of wood can clog up its nostrils, which are located at the base of its beak. The little bush of feathers helps keep out the bits of wood, but it can get awfully messy during cold and flu season.

## Cranes vs. Herons

*Dear Bird Folks:*

*A month ago I saw two very large birds fly out of the upper branches of a tree. As they flew they gave off a call that sounded like a rusty car door opening. Most notable was the shape of their necks, which looked like the trap under my kitchen sink. Could these have been cranes? Do cranes live in these parts?*

—*Joe,* WAYLAND, MA

Hey, Joe,

You wouldn't happen to be a plumber, would you? I get a lot of odd bird descriptions, but this is the first one that has incorporated parts of the kitchen sink. Before I could answer this question, I had to climb underneath my kitchen sink so I could understand what you were talking about. And let me tell you, Joe, I'm never doing that again. Talk about gross. Now, I know what the mice have been complaining about.

As odd as your description of the birds was, it was accurate. You did a great job of describing your bird; unfortunately, you didn't describe a crane. Although we do occasionally see cranes around here, seeing two would be almost unheard of. Equally unheard of is having cranes flying out of the tops of trees. Cranes have no use for trees. When not flying, they have their feet firmly planted on the ground. You would have a better chance of seeing a poodle fly out of a tree than a crane. Also, the voice of a crane is not at all like a rusty car door. It sounds more like a rusty bugle. Finally, cranes do not fly with their necks resembling any part of a kitchen sink. They fly with their necks looking like a two-inch piece of copper tubing. I'm not sure what that means; I was just trying to talk like a plumber. Anyhow, cranes fly with their necks straight out, like, um, a crane.

The bird you described is our old pal, the Great Blue Heron. Herons can be found just about anywhere there is water, including Wayland. Herons love trees. They even nest in trees. Their voice is a harsh squawk, doing justice to your rusty car door comparison. And because the heron's neck, bill, and head are disproportionately heavier than its body, it must rest them on its shoulders during flight. In order to fly, herons collapse their necks, giving them that S shape, or as you plumbers say, the "kitchen sink trap" look. The odd part about this whole thing is that many people call the sink trap a "goose neck," when in fact geese, like cranes, fly with their necks straight. "Heron neck" would be a more accurate name. Somebody needs to look into getting that changed and trademarked.

Here in North America, we have two types of native cranes: the very rare Whooping Crane and the very common Sandhill Crane. Both are found in the western states, with smaller populations occurring in the Deep South. The majestic Whooping Crane, the largest wading bird in North America, was all but wiped off the face of the earth by the 1940s. The population had dropped to only fifteen birds when a massive effort was made to save them. Now, over sixty years later, with a wild population of only about two hundred, this wonderful bird still hovers on the brink. The Sandhill Crane, on the other hand, is doing quite well. Waves of them can be seen along their migration routes through the middle of North America. Sandhills are so common in some areas that thousands of them are legally shot for the entertainment of grown adults. Go figure.

Sorry to spoil your crane sighting, Joe, but don't give up looking. Just about every year someone spots a crane somewhere in New England. Keep looking at every field you see and who knows, you might find a crane someday. Just don't look for cranes on the tops of trees. They won't ever be there. And no matter what you do, don't look for anything under my kitchen sink. You'll be scarred for life.

## King Fish It Isn't

*Dear Bird Folks:*
*The other day a bird flew across the pond near my house. It was*
*making a loud, harsh call. My aunt told me that it was a "King*
*Fish." Are they common around here?*

—*Joan,* OAK HILL, WV

Well, Joan,
The bird that you saw was a "kingfisher," not a "king fish." Your aunt was close but she must be having flashbacks of the old *Amos 'n' Andy* shows.

The Belted Kingfisher is one of the coolest birds you'll ever see. And yes, they are fairly common in West Virginia. I really get a kick out of kingfishers because they seem to hate everybody and everything. They are like a flying badger, always in a bad mood. They hate things they haven't met yet. You've got to respect a creature like that.

Their call is a loud, harsh, dry rattle that can be heard at great distances. If you happen to come upon a perched kingfisher, it will immediately take off, cursing you and your entire family as it flies away. Some scientists have said an English translation of the kingfisher's call is "#*&@!" but this has never been proven. Even when they are courting, kingfishers sound nasty. I watched a pair courting a few weeks ago and the whole time they screamed at each other. It was like listening to a pair of lawyers on a date.

Kingfishers can be found throughout most of the U.S. and southern Canada. They are always near water and as their name implies, they eat mostly fish, which they hunt from the air. Hovering like terns, kingfishers dive headfirst into the water with a huge splash. They then fly to their favorite perch for lunch, cursing all the way.

One of the most unique things about kingfishers is their nesting behavior. Kingfishers nest in underground burrows, like gophers. They make six-foot-long tunnels in the sides of sand cliffs or dirt banks. At the end of the tunnel they build a large, round chamber where they lay their eggs. Both the male and female kingfishers work on building these long tunnels, which can be dug at a rate of a foot a day, making the kingfisher the favorite bird of prisoners everywhere.

So, Joan, keep your eyes and ears open anytime you are near water. You are bound to see and hear a kingfisher. Just don't try to make friends with it because it hates you and there ain't nothing you can do about it.

## Bloodcurdling Screams in the Night

*Dear Bird Folks:*

*I live in what some people might call "the country." It's an area of back roads, farms, and woods. After dinner, I take long power walks through abandoned fields and on back roads. I am very used to the sounds of the night. Coyote howls, owl hoots, and raccoon growls don't bother me at all. That all changed two weeks ago. While cutting through a farmer's field, I heard the worst sound I have ever heard in my life. The best way to describe it is a bloodcurdling scream. It totally creeped me out. Then, a few nights later I heard it again. Now I take my walks someplace else. Do you have any idea what made that awful sound: bird, mammal, alien?*

*—Paul, HAYS, KS*

You big baby, Paul,

You mean to tell me that late at night while you are walking alone in the dark, along some deserted field, you hear an unidentifiable bloodcurdling scream and this somehow makes you uncomfortable? What kind of a wimp are you? What are you worried about? You said you were taking a "power walk." Everybody knows that nothing can hurt you when you are power walking. Look it up in your Personal Safety Handbook. You'll see.

In order to identify your mystery screamer, we have to narrow down our choices. I doubt the scream came from an alien because an alien's call is usually a series of short phrases, followed by, "Nanu, nanu, this is Mork calling Orson." What you heard was no alien. It also couldn't have been a mammal because I don't write about mammals. That leaves us with some kind of bird. There, that didn't take us long to narrow things down.

In the fall many birds are migrating at night and they call to each other while they are flying. On a calm, clear fall night you could hear migrating songbirds, waterfowl, even shorebirds. But none of them give a bloodcurdling scream . . . unless the bird flying in front of them suddenly stops short. Owls would be a good possibility. I know you said that you were familiar with the hoots of an owl, but not all owls hoot. Actually, most owls don't hoot. They also don't all scream either, but one owl sure does. I'm betting that you have been hearing the calls of the Barn Owl, and if it was, I can totally understand why you would never want to leave your house again.

You were correct in describing the Barn Owl's calls as bloodcurdling. It's hard to imagine an eerier call in all of nature. Banshees sound like nightingales compared to the call of a Barn Owl. They are not only scary to hear, they can be even scarier to see. Barn Owls are slender with white undersides. When seen flying at night, they resemble ghostly spirits. That's not something you want to see when you are walking alone in the dark.

Late one night, a friend and I were driving down a lonely stretch of highway in Arizona. Along the side of the road were many white crosses. Talk about being creeped out. We weren't sure if something awful had happened on this road or the locals were simply trying to ward off vampires. Either way, the crosses put us on edge. Then, out of the darkness, a white image flew across the road, over the hood, and in front of the windshield of our car. They could have heard our screams in Madagascar, with the windows closed. I quickly realized that we had just seen a Barn Owl on its evening hunt, and a smile came upon my face. My friend, on the other hand, is entering his fourth year of therapy.

You have nothing to fear from a Barn Owl. When seen during the day they are rather sweet looking, for an owl. They have heart-shaped faces and are not at all menacing. Barn owls actually like people and as their name implies, live in our barns and other empty buildings. Farmers love them because they eat tons of rodents. Some people have even put up Barn Owl nesting boxes with some success. I know their raspy, screechy calls are tough to take, but your voice might be a bit harsh too if you swallowed a whole rat every day of your life.

Instead of avoiding the area where you heard those mystery calls, Paul, I think you should go back there. If you take along a strong flashlight, you might get lucky and see the ghostly form of the Barn Owl winging across the fields on its evening hunt. And, if for some reason I'm wrong and those awful screams aren't coming from an owl, forget what I said about power walking and try some serious power running instead.

## Red vs. Gray Owls

*Dear Bird Folks:*
*Last year I had a gray screech owl in a nest box in my yard. This*
*year the bird is back, only this time it looks red. I've read that*
*screech owls have a red and gray morph. Could this be last year's*
*bird in a red morph?*

—*Yolanda,* DENNIS, MA

Yo, Yolanda,

You get points for being the first person to ask a question
using the word "morph." It shows you've been reading your bird
books. You are also the first Yolanda to ever write to us. You don't
get points for that. I just thought you should know.

For the rest of you non-readers, morph refers to a color varia-
tion in birds. A color morph should not be confused with seasonal or breeding colors. A male goldfinch is not entering a new
color morph when he molts into his bright yellow summer
plumage. A color morph is permanent and not related to age,
sex, season, religion, or voting record. Different-colored birds of
the same species are not common, although it does happen
(pigeons, for instance).

The red owl that you are seeing this year, Yolanda, is not the
gray owl you had in your nest box last year. Screech owls come in
two basic color phases: red and gray. There is a less common
brown phase found mostly in Florida and a much rarer paisley
phase, but those birds haven't been seen since the late sixties.

A red-colored owl will always be red and a gray owl will always
be gray . . . unless it goes somewhere to have the gray touched up.
The interesting thing about screech owls is that a pair can produce a family of all red or all gray or a mixture of some red and
some gray owlets. And, being totally liberal in their thinking, red
and gray owls seem to have no issues about interbreeding.

However, their offspring will either be red or gray, not some weird third color.

Screech owls like to nest in tree cavities, but will readily come to properly sized bird boxes. What's neat about screech owls is that they will also use nest boxes to roost in during the non-breeding season. On a cold winter's day the owls can often be seen sitting in the entry hole sunning themselves. Many people report that roosting screech owls are rather tame in the winter, allowing close approach. Yet, they become fearless and aggressive in the breeding season if their nest is approached and have no problem taking the toupee right off your head.

Screech owls are fairly small, not much larger than a baked potato. They are the smallest owls with ear tufts in the East and that sometimes fools nearsighted people into believing they are seeing a baby Great Horned Owl.

Screech owls are late night owls that are more often heard than seen. They can be heard calling any time of year, but spring and fall are the most common. Their call is not really a screech but more of a descending whinny that reminds me of a tiny horse. But I might be alone on that one.

Since they are little owls, their prey is also small. These guys eat mostly frogs, worms, beetles, and small mammals such as mice and shrews. Finding food can lead to problems for these owls. Hunting in the open makes them vulnerable to becoming dinner for larger owls. Also, screech owls will sometimes pick worms off a wet road, putting them in danger of morphing into a hood ornament on a passing Buick.

Congratulations on your owls, Yolanda. Hopefully, they will build a nest. If they do raise a family, run out and fill your feeder full of fresh shrews. I think Stop & Shop carries them but don't buy the frozen or Tex-Mex shrews; the owls don't seem to like them as much.

147

# 7.

## The Off-Season

Much like gardening, backyard bird watching has become a springtime activity that helps signal the end of winter: hummingbird feeders are put out; birdbaths are dragged up from the basement; birdhouses are opened up and cleaned, in hopes of attracting new families. Spring is an exciting time for both birders and gardeners. But unlike plants, when fall arrives birds don't dry up and go to seed. Most birds are forced to pack up and leave, while some remain where they hatched out. The challenges migrating birds meet on their long flights are many, but it's no picnic for the birds that stay behind either. They must face the winter head-on. I get the chills just thinking of a songbird, with the body weight of a potato chip, surviving night after night in subzero weather. Bird migration and winter survival are topics most of us would rather ignore, but a few nosy people out there need to know the answers to everything. Luckily for me, those answers aren't as boring as they sound.

## Missing Feeder Birds

*Dear Bird Folks:*
*For the past few weeks I have had almost no birds coming to my*
*feeders. We always get tons of birds. Has something happened*
*to them?*

—*Tim,* UTICA, NY

No offense, Tim,

But every December I get this question about six hundred times a day. And every December I write about it, but either no one is reading this or whoever does read it quickly forgets what I've written. Either way, I'm a little hurt. However, for you, Tim, I'll answer this question one more time. Just do me a favor. Please cut the answer out and stick it on your refrigerator. Or better yet, tape it to your forehead so when the next person asks me, I can simply point them in your direction.

There are fewer birds at our feeders in December because there are fewer birds in the northern regions. It's that migration thing. Some of the biggest flying pigs have gone south. We seem to have fewer small birds, such as House Finches, in the winter, but the bird whose absence really has an impact is the grackle. Grackles not only eat from our feeders, but chow down tons of natural food that other feeder birds like to eat. Without grackles, more birdseed and natural food becomes available for the birds that remain here all winter.

Speaking of natural food and feeders, December is one of the most bountiful months of the year for natural food. Many seeds and berries become available to birds in late fall. This is also the time of year when many "old school" bird-feeding people dig their feeders out of the basement for their seasonal feeding program. The abundant natural food and additional feeders combine to offer way too many choices to the smaller winter population of birds.

Now, Tim, the next thing you are supposed to say (because everyone else does) is, "But this has never happened to me before." And when you say that, try to put some contempt in your voice. Yes, it has happened before. It happens every year. Perhaps not to you but it does happen. This is just your turn. In nature, things rarely happen exactly the same way twice, except in the case of Old Faithful and Elvis impersonators.

There is one more part of this equation that I have yet to mention and this could have an even more dramatic effect on the birds at your feeders. Hawks. Small-bird-eating Cooper's and Sharp Shinned Hawks often plague backyards in the winter. These fast hawks love to eat feeder birds. A visit from one of these hawks can cause small birds to avoid your yard like golfers avoid exercise.

What can you do? Moving your feeders to a sheltered area will offer the birds some protection from those hawks. Will your birds come back? Of course they will, just as soon as we get some nasty weather and the natural food becomes harder to find. In the meantime, make sure the food in your feeder stays dry. Uneaten seed can become pretty rotten after sitting outside in a feeder for weeks at a time. Spoiled seed is harmful to birds, so keep your food fresh. When the birds finally do return, if your seed is wet and moldy, they'll take one bite and leave again . . . only this time they'll be talking about you.

## Bird Migration: Gotta Go Now

*Dear Bird Folks:*
*I recently saw a TV show on bird migration and have become*
*very interested in the subject. I would like you to write something*
*about bird migration.*

—*Bill,* MANCHESTER, CT

Something's missing, Bill,

You wrote, "I would like you to write something . . ." Where is
the question? Haven't you noticed that this is a question and
answer format? This is not *The Request Hour.* Here's how it works.
Someone asks me a question. I then consult with the world's top
scientists and formulate a precise answer. Without a specific question, I don't know what to write about. I guess I could make up a
question but my head is so jam-packed with answers I don't have
any room left for questions. All right, let me see what I can do.

You are right to be interested in bird migration. It is by far one
of the most amazing events in all of nature. It is not quite as amazing as the guy who ate fifty hot dogs in twelve minutes on ESPN a
few weeks ago, but it's close. The ability of birds of all sizes—from
massive cranes to minute hummingbirds—to migrate thousands
of miles has intrigued scientists for centuries. Why birds migrate,
how they store enough food for the trip, and how they find their
way are important questions, Bill. They would have been good
ones for you to ask.

Why birds migrate seems like an easy one to answer. Who
wouldn't want to avoid a New England winter to spend time in the
sunny tropics? But that doesn't explain why they leave the tropics
in the first place. Why would a bird fly 1,000 miles north to build
a nest, when it could simply build a nest where it has been spending the winter? The answers to that question are many but much

of it has to do with overcrowding. By flying north, birds can exploit the wide-open, food-rich, bug-infested wilds of Canada.

The North Country provides excellent breeding grounds, which produce millions of new baby birds. It is with these brand-new birds that migration really becomes amazing. Think about this for a minute or even a second. Baby birds, not much more than a month or so old, somehow have to find their way to the wintering grounds. Often, they do it without the help of the parents, a map, or a Fodor's guide. At first, the newly hatched birds are having the best time playing with their fellow nestlings or practicing their flying skills. Then suddenly, they are struck with a case of Zugunruhe. ("Zugunruhe" means "migratory restlessness," for all of you out there who are weak on your German crossword puzzle words.)

Instantly, the fun is gone and the birds start to get antsy. They eat constantly, nearly doubling their weight. Then, late one night, when the weather conditions are just right, they step into the night sky, all alone. Flying away from the only world that they have ever known, the little birds head off into the pitch dark for a place they've never been before. Is it me, or is this starting to sound like a John Denver song?

By using the stars and directions they inherited from their parents, the birds stream south. Some birds make short flights, stopping along the way to refuel, while others fly nonstop. It's these nonstop flights that astonish me. For example, Blackpoll Warblers will take off from Nova Scotia and fly hundreds of miles out over the Atlantic Ocean. They then take a right turn east of Bermuda and continue straight to South America, never stopping once. These little birds, about the size and weight of a marshmallow, don't have food, water, or a second of rest for eighty-six hours. Wow! I'd like to see that hot-dog-eating ESPN guy do that.

When the warblers finally do land, they are nothing more than flying skeletons, totally depleted of all body fat. If they are lucky, the ravaged birds will find food and a place to rest the moment they land in South America. But if Club Med has turned their wintering grounds into yet another golf course, these birds are in big trouble.

In the North, creatures that don't migrate either have to endure long periods of frigid weather or hibernate like bears. The problem with hibernation is the ones that do it miss out on all those great winter holidays. Migration is really the way to go. But migration isn't an option for all creatures. And it's lucky for us that it isn't. Florida has enough trouble right now without dealing with thousands of Grizzly Bears looking for a place to hang all winter.

Bird migration is as diverse as it is amazing. The lazy cardinal pretty much stays in the same area year round. Birds like Snowy Owls only migrate when there is a shortage of food while others, like Bobolinks, can't get far enough away from here; they fly all the way to Argentina.

The most ambitious bird of them all is the Arctic Tern. This small tern, measuring fifteen inches long and weighing a mere four ounces, nests mostly in the high Arctic but likes to spend its winters way down in Antarctica. In the late summer, it leaves North America for its long journey south. You would think that to save time and energy, it would head directly south. But nooo . . . this crazy bird flies east, way east, all the way across the ocean to Europe. Then it works its way along the coast to Africa and finally on to Antarctica. By the time the tern returns in the spring, it will have flown nearly 35,405 kilometers. I'm not really sure how far that is in miles, but I bet it's a lot.

Equally as diverse is the time of day that birds make their flights. There are birds that only travel at night, some that only fly during the day, and others that don't seem to care when they fly. Most songbirds fly at night, which is unusual since the rest of the year they don't fly after sunset. The cover of darkness protects them from songbird-loving hawks and falcons. Birds of prey, on the other hand, migrate during the day. They depend on the heat of the sun to warm up air pockets, called "thermals." Hawks can soar on thermals for miles without flapping a wing. Ducks and geese migrate either day or night, probably depending on the amount of coffee they drank at breakfast.

Nighttime songbird migration fooled many early scientists. Since the birds were there one day and gone the next, they figured they must be hibernating nearby in some secret underground location. Other naturalists believed that birds would simply fly off to the moon for the winter. The moon? I wonder what those guys were smoking. For years, many thought that hummingbirds were not strong enough to fly across the Gulf of Mexico on their own. They believed that hummingbirds rode across the Gulf on the backs of larger birds, like cranes or geese. Can you imagine flying across the Gulf on the back of a goose? The honking alone would make the hummers wish they had taken a bus.

A combination of length of day, temperature, and weather helps to trigger migration. (More of this riveting bird migration discussion may be found on page 192. Talk about something to look forward to.) When all of the conditions line up just right, the birds make their move. Huge waves of them go for it at the same time. Radar has detected as many as fifteen million birds flying over Cape Cod on a single fall night. Can you imagine fifteen million birds overhead? That would be the wrong night to forget to take your laundry off the clothesline.

For those of you who don't have your own radar, here is something fun you can try. About 11 P.M. on a clear, moonlit September night, focus your spotting scope (binoculars might work, too) on the moon. You'll be surprised how many birds you will see blasting past the moon on their way south. (That's *past* the moon, not *to* it.) I tried this last year and it actually worked. I could see hundreds of silhouettes, thousands of feet up in the night sky, racing toward a very distant destination. Give it a try. If the birds don't show up and you get bored, you can always use your spotting scope to see what your neighbor is doing after 11 at night.

In the meantime, practice saying "Zugunruhe." You know you want to.

## Feeders Won't Stop Hummingbird Migration

*Dear Bird Folks:*
*I know you are probably sick of answering questions about hum-mingbirds, but I really need to know the answer to this question soon. For the second year in a row, my neighbor has warned me to take down my hummingbird feeder. He said that feeding hum-mingbirds late in the season will encourage them to remain here, not migrate south, and they could die when winter arrives. Is any of this true? Should I take my feeders down?*

—*Tess,* ALTON, NH

No, no, no, Tess,

I'm not sick of writing about hummingbirds. I love humming-birds. Okay, maybe I am getting a little sick of writing about them, but what I really am really getting sick of is neighbors with bad advice. Nosy neighbors. Has there ever been a dopier group of people? In fact, according to the latest *USA Today* poll, the nosy neighbor has moved into first place, overtaking in-laws as the number one provider of misinformation. Now, that's saying something.

To begin with, hummingbird migration is different than the migration of many other birds. There are no massive flocks of hummingbirds gathering on the power lines like swallows, swarms descending into the marshes like blackbirds, or long Vs streaming across the fall sky like geese.

Hummingbirds migrate alone. The truth is hummingbirds hate each other. They don't need a large flock of other hummers acting like nosy neighbors telling them when it's time to leave or gathered around for protection. They are plenty streetwise and can handle themselves. The other thing is that these independent birds don't even head south at the same time; some go early, some go later. Their migration is drawn out over several months. Are you wondering why, Tess?

Unlike most songbirds, hummingbirds don't pair up as long-term couples. The male and female hook up briefly to mate and then go their separate ways. (I told you they hated each other.) The female builds the nest, lays the eggs (you may have already guessed that part), sits on the eggs, and hatches and raises the entire brood all by herself. The only thing the male does is mate and that's it. As part of nature's payback for making them so small, male hummingbirds are allowed to mate with as many females as they can attract. Once their "work" is done and all the females are busy tending the nests, the males get bored and start thinking about heading back down south, probably to rest.

Hummingbird migration may start as early as late July for the males, and will continue into October for the females and young birds. If your neighbor's statement was true, in order to avoid disrupting migration, you would have to take your feeder down in July. Heck, in New Hampshire, most people haven't even finished digging their feeders out of the snow banks until July.

It is certainly safe to assume that our feeders benefit the hummingbirds, but what they really depend on are flowers. Hummingbirds feed off both the nectar flowers provide and the minute insects attracted to them. Tons of flowers, both wild and cultivated, are in full bloom in late summer. Why would the birds leave when there is so much natural food around? Because they know the big chill is coming. Migratory instincts are much too strong to be swayed by a few posies. Neither flowers nor feeders are going to keep the hummers from getting out while the getting is good.

Every year some hummingbird somewhere ends up at a feeder long after it should have gone south. Newspapers love to print pictures of a confused hummingbird at a feeder in December. The suggestion by some people (usually a neighbor) is that the artificial food supply discouraged the bird from migrating. Well, the reality is the late bird probably did migrate but it went the wrong way. Occasionally, birds get their brain wires crossed and they migrate north or east instead of south and become lost. Just like some people (usually a neighbor) who drive the wrong way down a one-way street. It happens.

You can leave your hummingbird feeder out as long as you'd like, Tess. Your bird feeder will not interfere with bird migration. However, it will sometimes help keep a lost bird alive, at least for a while. Sadly, the migration instinct only lasts for a short while. Even the onset of cold weather won't force a bird that has strayed to move on; eventually, it will have to deal with the unforgiving winter. Nature has a rather harsh way of taking the misfits out of the gene pool. Too bad nature doesn't take the nosiness out of the neighborhood.

## When Barn Swallows Finally
## Leave the Barn

*Dear Bird Folks:*
*For many years we have welcomed Barn Swallows to our small*
*barn. We keep at least one door open for them to fly in and out*
*of. They pay us back by eating untold numbers of flying insects.*
*Then suddenly they are gone, leaving nothing but messy nests.*
*Where do they go?*

—*Mert,* BREWSTER, MA

Good for you, Mert,

Good for you for keeping your barn door open for the swallows. It is hard to find a sweeter bird than a Barn Swallow, but you
would not believe the number of complaints I get about them. All
spring I receive calls from whiners, wondering how they can keep
swallows *out* of their barn or shed. They moan, "The bird droppings are making a mess." I reply, "Dude, it's a barn, not an operating room. Barns are supposed to be a little messy. That's what
makes them barns. Get over it." I don't have many friends.

Of the six species of swallows that breed in the eastern U.S.,
the Barn Swallow is the one with the stereotypical swallowtail. Its
long, forked tail gives the birds excellent maneuverability in flight
and gives us a handy field mark for identification. Like other swallows, the Barn Swallow has suffered from our love affair with pesticides. Yet, by incorporating their nesting colonies into many of
our buildings, they have also benefited from us.

For the rest of us who don't have nesting Barn Swallows, let
me explain a bit about their nests. The nest is a cup made entirely of straw and mud. When nest-building swallows discover a mud
puddle, a frenzy ensues, much like a bunch of Atkins freaks at a
steak house. The twittering swallows descend from all over, scooping up delicious mud in their bills. Up to a thousand beakfuls of

mud may be needed to complete a nest, after which the swallows have to spend a lot of time gargling and flossing.

It is believed that swallows spend more time on the wing than any other songbird, flying the equivalent of six hundred miles a day searching for food. As their name indicates, upon finding food they swallow it. There is no biting, chewing, or stashing it for later; the food instantly goes down the hatch.

Unlike a bunch of deadbeat relatives, swallows are hardly free-loaders; they earn their keep. Swallows pay for their rental space by eating huge amounts of insects, including beetles, bees, flying ants, houseflies, and horse flies.

When food is plentiful, the young birds grow quickly and are out of the nest in about two weeks. It is their last few days in the nest that causes the mess that freaks some people out. When the babies are small, the parents carry away the droppings in neat packages, called "fecal sacks." But as the kids get older and stronger, they simply raise their bums up and over the rim of the nest and let it rip.

Unlike Tree Swallows, which can survive on bayberries, Barn Swallows eat nearly 100 percent insects, so they need to be long gone before cold weather arrives. By the middle of August, most Barn Swallows start to head out. Hundreds of them can be seen on power lines, flocking up for the long migration. At sunset, huge flocks of swallows descend into nearby marshes to roost for the night. The sight of hundreds of birds diving into a marsh made early Europeans think that swallows spent the winter buried in marsh mud. Pretty silly idea, but what else would you expect from the people who thought the earth was flat and who drive Renaults?

At first light the flock starts the long trip south. Covering several hundred miles a day, the swallows are focused on reaching their wintering grounds in South America. Some birds arrive via Mexico and Central America, while others island hop across the

West Indies. The island hoppers have the shortest route but are also at the mercy of the weather. Hurricanes and tropical storms take a toll on migrating birds by battering them with wind, rain, and flying nuns.

By the time you read this, Mert, your swallows will be well on their way to a winter of fun and sun in South America. I'm sorry to hear that they left your barn such a mess. If I were you, I would withhold their security deposit. That will teach them.

## Goldfinches Aren't Always Gold

*Dear Bird Folks:*
*I seem to have lost all of my male goldfinches. My feeders are full of dull-looking females. What's happened to all the males?*
*—Martha, BURLINGTON, VT*

Martha, my dear,
Your male goldfinches are not lost; in fact, they haven't even left your yard. Male goldfinches are still coming to your feeder, except recently they have started dressing like females. Yes, even birds have intriguing habits.

Fall is a time of molting for most birds. With the upcoming winter, worn feathers need to be replaced for added protection against the nasty weather and to keep up with the latest trends. In some bird species, the molt is dramatic; with others, it's hard to even tell they've ever molted. Chickadees, for example, know that gray is a hot color and stick with it day in and day out, all year long, even through the molt. They look the same from the day they first fly until the day they die. Other birds look like totally different creatures after they molt. Their bright, sparkling summer colors are long gone and are replaced with colors that are so drab the birds look like little UPS employees.

The male American Goldfinch falls into that latter group. He shines all summer in his brilliant yellow and black colors, but in the fall he molts into a drab olive, looking much like a female. Why do they change colors at all? The reasons that we hear most have to do with mate attraction and camouflage. A full-colored male will be more likely to catch the eye of the ladies in the spring, while turning dull in the fall will help the bird hide more easily from its enemies.

That seems to make some sense but it doesn't explain the year-round flashy colors of Blue Jays, bluebirds, and male Northern Cardinals. They seem to do just fine, even in winter, without molting into some generic camouflage color. Speaking of generic, what about sparrows? They never get flashy. They never change out of their dreary wardrobe. Yet, judging from their abundance, they don't have trouble finding any action during breeding season.

In nature, like everything else, nothing succeeds like success. Whether it is generic or seasonally fancy plumage, it's all about what works. Changing colors twice a year works for American Goldfinches and they aren't about to give that up. What is really impressive is that they are the radicals of the finch world. They are the only ones in their family that change colors spring and fall; the rest can't be bothered and stay the same year round.

Don't worry, Martha. Next spring your male goldfinches will once again be all pimped out in their bright mating colors, just as they have been for thousands of years. If you happen to see a dull goldfinch in the summer, it will either be a female or a male finch that has taken a delivery job with UPS.

## Birds Aren't Big Fans of Hurricanes

*Dear Bird Folks:*
*Last week I had both orioles and hummingbirds still coming to*
*my feeders. Suddenly I don't see either one. Do you think it is the*
*threat of this hurricane that has made both birds leave so quick-*
*ly? Also, I'm worried what this big storm will do to all of the birds*
*that are moving south this time of year. Are they in trouble?*
*—Joyce,* CRANSTON, RI

You're sweet, Joyce,

With everyone running around buying batteries, masking tape, and bottled water in preparation for this storm, you are very thoughtful to be worrying about the birds. And you should be worried; a hurricane can be tough on birds and just about everything else in its path. Hummingbirds and orioles are no match for a storm that can flatten full-sized buildings.

However, the reason your hummingbirds and orioles have moved on has nothing to do with the weather report. Unless you are somebody who watches The Weather Channel really loud, the birds in your yard have no idea about any big storm coming. Birds are sensitive to certain climatic changes, but right now the storm that has you and everyone else worried is several hundred miles away. Only people and creatures with expanded basic cable have knowledge of this storm.

Your hummers and orioles have left because it's time for them to go. Even though the weather is still warm and there is plenty of food around, they must leave. Central America is the place these birds call home in the off-season, and there is no way they want to experience a New England winter.

You might not realize it but "your" hummingbirds and orioles probably moved out weeks ago. The birds that have been at your feeders recently are more than likely birds that were hatched out in northern New England or Canada. They are using your feeders as a refueling stop on the long trip south.

As noted above, birds can sense climatic changes. After refueling, they wait for favorable weather conditions. Most like to ride the leading edge of cold fronts, which often provide the proper tailwinds needed for long flights. Moving fronts at night are especially beneficial to songbirds. Nighttime air is often less turbulent than air that has been heated by the sun. That is why your birds seem to be here one day and gone the next . . . because that is exactly what happens.

Hurricanes—like any kind of bad weather—do cause big problems for migrating birds. Birds flying over land can settle down and ride out the storm huddled up, but birds caught over the open ocean are in big trouble. If they are unable to fly above or around the storm, they become exhausted and are soon headed for a date with SpongeBob.

Although it is sad to think about birds being lost at sea, it's important to remember that not all birds migrate at the same time. Any given storm will stop only a small percentage of migrating birds. The real problem with hurricanes is the damage they cause to environmentally sensitive areas. Tidal surges wash over barrier beaches that can take years to recover. Flooding rains can dilute brackish marshes, wiping out critical feeding areas. And, of course, the wind damage to trees, shrubs, and other vegetation can eliminate thousands of acres of nesting habitat.

I'm glad you are concerned about the birds' safety, Joyce. I'd write more about this subject but I need to run out for some batteries, masking tape, and bottled water.

## Desperate Winter Robins

*Dear Bird Folks:*
*From years of reading your columns, I have become aware that seeing robins in the winter is no big deal. Still, I wasn't prepared for the massive number of robins that descended upon my yard after a bad storm a few weeks ago. I wanted to do something for them, but we were plumb out of fresh worms. Why had so many robins come to my yard in particular and was there anything that I could have done to help those fat, shivering birds?*

—*Mary,* NJ

You weren't alone, Mary,

I'd be willing to bet that following that storm, over 90 percent of the calls, letters, faxes, e-mails, and encrypted messages from other worlds were from people who were getting flocks of robins in their yards. Every person I saw, whether it was a customer or just some stalker on the street, would ask, "What can I do for the robins?" Apparently, robins spent the days following the blizzard in every yard in the Northeast. When things are bad the birds look for any port in a storm, even if it's in New Jersey.

You were right when you said that seeing American Robins in the winter is no big deal. If you looked at a winter range map, you would see that robins may be found year round across nearly the entire country. The one exception is northern New England, which they often bypass in order to avoid being run over by snow-mobiles. You may have heard this before, but many of the robins we see in the winter are those tough robins from Canada. A cold day for our robins feels like an afternoon in Fort Lauderdale to those Canadian birds.

Robins are stout, hardy birds that can handle just about any weather if they are able to find enough food. Their ability to find food is the key to their nationwide presence. As with all creatures, the more varied their diet, the more successful the species. It is the creatures with specialized feeding habits that suffer in tough times. That's one reason why unicorn-eating hawks have been looking so thin recently.

If the ground is soft, robins happily dig for bugs or delicious slimy worms. But when the earth is frozen, their food of choice becomes fruit and berries. We see few robins in a mild winter. They are around but spend much of their time in moist woodlands eating wild berries. When deep snow covers the food, the robins head to the neighborhoods. What are robins looking for in our yards? Anything they can get their beaks on. The more severe the weather, the less fussy the birds. They'll eat just about any kind of berries or fruit, with most of it being swallowed whole, although whole pineapples are only swallowed when things are really bad.

Even though robins are a common yard bird, they could hardly be called a common feeder bird. But after that last blizzard just about every yard in the East had robins picking at something. We had calls from people who had robins fighting woodpeckers at the suet feeder and some that were clinging to tube feeders, chowing down sunflower seed. And in one instance, a robin was seen dropping quarters into a vending machine to get a package of gummy worms. The irate bird was seen later in the day kicking the machine when it realized the worms were candy.

Even desperate robins aren't always willing to come to feeders. The best we can do for them is to put out a variety of foods. Based on feedback from customers, raisins and currants seem to be the most popular choices. Some people soak them in water first, while others don't. Robins may eat other fruit, like blueberries or small grapes. As an experiment, I lined the railing of my deck with large, frozen blueberries. The birds didn't eat them but the squirrels were thrilled, and the berries left lovely stains on my railing. No good deed goes unpunished.

Other foods to try are suet chopped up on a tray, and sun-flower seeds without the shells. Even bakery goods have reported-ly been eaten by hungry robins. However, I'd avoid offering bran muffins if you aren't in the mood to wash your windows.

Finally, Mary, you should know that robins and bluebirds are in the same family, so whatever works to attract robins should work for bluebirds. Putting out any of the aforementioned foods, plus mealworms and fresh water, could also get you a flock of bluebirds. But whatever you do, don't offer gummy worms or you might find yourself being kicked in the shins by an angry robin or irate bluebird.

## Birdhouses Aren't Just for Nesting Anymore

*Dear Bird Folks:*
*I've heard that birds will use nesting boxes to roost in during the*
*colder months. Would it be a good idea to put out more boxes in*
*the winter? Also, do birds roost in flocks, and if so are the flocks*
*mixed or do the birds only roost with the same species?*

—*Roy,* CHATHAM, MA

Hey, Roy,

Can we talk? So many gossipy questions about who birds sleep
with. Maybe I should pass this question on to Joan Rivers or whoever has taken Ann Landers's place. I'm certainly not going to ask
Hedda Hopper. She's still mad at me for passing her some bad
dirt about a Lady Bird Johnson. How was I supposed to know she
wasn't a real bird?

Roosting in cavities is one of the many survival techniques birds have developed to endure winter's bitter cold. By curling up in the hollow of a tree, birds are able to protect themselves from frigid winds. The interesting thing is that only a few birds have adopted this behavior; most sleep out under the stars. No matter how nasty the weather gets, you won't find birds like cardinals, Blue Jays, or mockingbirds hiding out in a rotted tree stump. They would rather freeze than crawl into a dark hollow that could be filled with scary spiders.

Typically, birds that roost in tree cavities are the same birds that nest in cavities. A bluebird that loves to build its nest in a birdhouse will also spend a cold winter night in a birdhouse. Meanwhile, the bluebird's cousin, the robin, has no use for any nesting box. Why? A scientist will tell you that it's all instinct, but I think it's because the robin is too darn fat and is afraid that it might get stuck in the hole.

Not all birds that roost in nesting cavities use them the same way. Some species are loners and will rarely shack up with any other bird, no matter how hot it looks. Much like an old married couple, a pair of Downy Woodpeckers may spend the entire day hanging out together, but at night they find it more peaceful to sleep alone. Tree Swallows, on the other hand, will pig pile into a cavity for some kind of wild group sleepover and not even ask first names. Other birds, like nuthatches, often sleep alone but will flock up when the weather gets extra cold. Creepers will do the same thing. I think we all know what it's like to wake up and find a creeper sleeping next to you.

From what I've read, Roy, it appears most birds that roost communally in cavities usually roost with their own species, i.e., bluebirds sleep with bluebirds, etc. I imagine some birds will occasionally mix things up and spend the night with a bird they aren't supposed to be with, but they don't talk about that much. In the bird world, image is everything.

What surprises me is that birds don't curl up at night with some sleeping mammal since that's where the heat is. Wouldn't a chickadee be better off cozying up to a snoozing bear than another shivering chickadee? Who knows, maybe some chickadees have tried to spend a night with a bear. If they have, they haven't made it back to tell anyone.

Many other birds also roost in flocks but they do so out in the cold. Crows and blackbirds form huge flocks. During the day, young birds follow the older birds around because adult birds are better at finding food. You would think that the older birds would scare off the younger birds in order to protect the food supply. But the adult birds know what they are doing because at night they sleep in the middle of the flock, forcing the kids to sleep on the outer edges. By staying in the middle, the older birds are protected from both the howling winds and hungry nocturnal predators. What a great plan. I need to try that the next time I take the family camping.

If you have several nesting boxes around your yard, Roy, you don't need to put up any extra for the winter, but you should clean out any old nests that remain from the summer. You can also purchase boxes that are specially made for roosting. Roosting boxes look much like regular nest boxes but they have a series of perches on the inside for birds to sleep on and the entry hole is near the bottom to help prevent heat loss. Just don't expect Lady Bird Johnson to be roosting in any of them. I was way off base with that.

## Little Birds Take on the Big Chill

*Dear Bird Folks:*
*Sitting here on this stormy night, by my cozy fire, makes me won-*
*der how birds survive this time of year. What do birds do when*
*the temperature and wind chill fall below zero?*

—*Gabriel,* TRURO, MA

They freeze, Gabriel,

That's what birds do when it gets too cold. Perhaps they don't freeze totally but it can be close. Although you would never know it by their cheery outward behavior, winter is a tough time for birds. When you think about it, the only thing that stands between a bird and the icy outside temperature is a ridiculously thin layer of feathers. If you took every feather off a chickadee and weighed them, the scale wouldn't move; a chickadee's total outer layer of protection weighs practically zero. I think the only thing that weighs less is the amount of common sense found on a federal tax form.

When it comes to dealing with winter, birds have two choices: head south or stay here and tough it out. After the weather we've had the last few years, heading south seems like a much better decision.

But migration is not always the best choice. Remember, birds don't pile into the back of a motor home and speed their way down I-95, counting "South of the Border" signs as they go. A trip south for birds is filled with all kinds of scary adventures. Birds have to deal with storms that blow them off course and cell towers that they can never seem to avoid. Plus, finding food in a habitat that is constantly disappearing is uncertain at best. Many birds that leave in the fall never make it back to see their breeding grounds again.

Yet as we all know, making it through a northern winter is no piece of cake either. Besides the extreme cold, food sources are often covered with snow and ice. Winter days are shorter, so there is less time to find food. Also, nights are longer and after dark is the hardest time for birds. With no food to provide energy and no sun to supply warmth, night for a bird can be a long time, almost as long as an afternoon watching golf on TV.

Birds use every trick they know to survive the night. Just like us, birds shiver to keep warm. They fluff out their feathers to trap more warm air. Some birds hunker down with other birds in birdhouses or woodpecker holes, sharing what little body heat they give off. Some birds will even bury themselves in the snow. Snow actually insulates them from the often colder air temperature. Dropping their own body temperature is another ability birds have that helps them survive. A chickadee can lower its nighttime temperature from one hundred and eight to ninety degrees in order to save energy and annoy the power company.

Birds also have minimal blood flow to their feet. A bird's body temperature may be over one hundred degrees but its feet may be just above freezing, which is a complaint I've heard about my own feet more than once. If somehow the fluffing and the shivering work and the bird is able to make it through the night, it is rewarded by having to do it all over again the next night.

Now, don't fret too much over this because it sounds worse than it is. Even though hard winter weather can push a bird's survival skills to the edge, birds are designed to be pushed to the edge. Most of the time a bird will return from the edge ready to take on the next challenge.

Enjoy your cozy fire, Gabriel. The birds can take care of themselves. But if you want to make yourself feel better and do something for them, put together a plate of cookies and a thermos of hot chocolate and leave them with me. I'll make sure they get it.

## Only Bird Watchers Would
## Even Think of Doing This

*Dear Bird Folks:*
*Last week I was walking on the beach with my black lab when I*
*came upon a group of bird watchers. Since the weather wasn't*
*very nice, I thought they must have come out to see some rare*
*bird. When I asked what was going on, they just replied,*
*"Christmas Count" and kept staring out at the water. Trying to*
*appear knowledgeable, I replied, "Oh," and kept walking down*
*the beach. What is this Christmas Count and why did so many*
*people need to be out there on such a nasty day?*

*—Jill,* BOSTON, MA

Come on, Jill,

Again with a dog? Recently, I had a question from another dog
walker. Is there some kind of national fad that I'm missing? Can't
anybody go outside anymore without having a dog with him or
her? Since your dog is a lab I sure hope it wasn't decked out in
one of those silly sweaters. Tell me it was wearing a lab coat
instead.

What you witnessed, Jill, is an annual event that started way
back when McKinley was president and has continued nonstop to
this day. The Christmas Bird Count has contributed tons of information to the world of science and natural history. And it is all
done by volunteers.

In the late 1800s, when thoughts about wildlife conservation
were as well received as Confederate money, some people would
spend Christmas Day participating in what was called a "side
hunt." The goal was to go out and shoot every creature wearing
fur or feathers. At the end of the day, whoever had the largest pile
of dead things was declared the winner. Nice, eh?

Then in the year 1900, along came ornithologist Frank Chapman, who through his magazine, *Bird Lore,* challenged people in Canada and the United States to go out on Christmas Day to count birds instead of shooting them. Evidently, counting birds on a cold winter's day sounded just as boring back then as it does now. Between the two countries, Frank was able to get only twenty-seven people, including him, to go out and count birds. But Frank wasn't about to give up and the count continued every Christmas Day from that day on.

Over one hundred years later, the count is going strong. Old Frank would be thrilled to learn that there are now close to 55,000 people—from Canada to South America—participating in his Christmas Bird Count. Although I'm not sure if people have become more environmentally concerned or they just want to get out of spending the entire day in the house with Aunt Martha.

The rules for counting are simple. Several groups of birders head out before sunrise to cover a predetermined fifteen-mile area. They count every single bird they see before the sun sets. At the end of the day, everyone who hasn't succumbed to frostbite gathers to add up all the birds that were seen.

Why, you ask? Why would anyone want to be outside all day counting birds and freezing? How bad can Aunt Martha be? The information gathered from these counts is invaluable. Since this count has been taking place, scientists have been able to identify bird population trends, both good and bad. Twenty years ago, the Christmas count did not find a single bluebird anywhere in Massachusetts; last year, over 1,700 were seen and that is clearly good news for bluebirds. Not all the trends are that positive, but we don't need to get into that right now. Let's not spoil what's left of the holidays.

More than thirty Christmas counts are held each year in Massachusetts, with several around Boston. And guess what, Jill?

You or anyone else can participate. (Relax, very few counts are held exactly on Christmas Day anymore. You'll still get to open your gifts.) All you need to do is sign up with an official organized group and dress warmly. Counts can be a lot of fun and, if you survive, very rewarding. And who knows, maybe you'll get lucky and meet someone else who can't go outside without having a dog with them. There sure doesn't seem to be any shortage of them these days.

# 8.

# Information Nobody
# Should Be Without

Having a birding business is much like running a roadside tourist information booth. We get the same questions over and over all day long. Only instead of people inquiring about where to eat lunch, buy cheap gas, or find the nearest restroom, birding shops are constantly asked how to attract cardinals, what is the correct formula for making hummingbird food, and where is the nearest restroom. Every once in a while, though, someone (who has probably just finished using the restroom) will come up with a fresh question. Some questions are intriguing and some are peculiar at best, but at least they give us something new to talk about (after the person leaves). "How fast do birds fly?" and "Why do they stand on one leg?" are legitimate questions. Some people, on the other hand, want the story behind why storks deliver babies or where birds sleep. Those people worry me.

## Why Don't Woodpeckers
## Get Headaches?

*Dear Bird Folks,*
*Do woodpeckers ever get headaches?*

—*Sandy, grade 7,* ORLEANS, MA

Hi, Sandy,

Although I've never thought about it, all that banging could give woodpeckers headaches. That would explain the suet-flavored aspirin I saw at CVS last week. You'd think they would get headaches from the way they pound on trees but, luckily for them, they have evolved a rather tough head. Much like a soccer player or a tall coal miner.

Actually, you are not the only one concerned about woodpecker migraines. One guy, Dr. Ivan Schwab, was so worried about the woodpeckers that he researched and wrote an extensive paper about this very topic. And, believe it or not, the good doctor received an Ig Nobel Prize for his efforts. If you don't know what that is, Sandy, don't sweat it; nobody else does either. The Ig Nobels are awards given for research done on topics that are so strange only university professors and seventh graders have enough time on their hands to worry about them.

Woodpeckers are among our most common backyard birds, yet they have features that are totally different than other feeder birds. Woodpeckers have developed a much larger brain case, which prevents the birds from getting a concussion every time they have to chop out lunch. They also have different muscle and bone structure at the base of the bill, which acts like a shock absorber to help cushion the blows. And the woodpecker's stiff, strong tail serves as a kickstand to prop the bird up, allowing it to lean back and smack the tree. Even woodpeckers' feet are different. Most feeder birds have three toes in the front and one in the back; however, most woodpeckers have two in the front and two in the back, giving the birds a better grip on the trunk of the tree. They even have special feathers that cover their nostrils to keep out flying woodchips and other assorted debris.

I know this is a little dull to read, Sandy, but you asked, and it's not about to get any better. The tongue of a woodpecker is its most unusual feature. Its extra-long tongue wraps around inside the back of the woodpecker's head. When the bird wants to reach deep into a tree for a tasty insect treat, it shoots out its tongue like one of those annoying party favors. The tongue is also barbed and sticky so it can grab on to bugs and yank them out of their hiding places. This useful tongue saves the bird a lot of work by allowing it to pull out food without having to chisel deeper into the tree. Hey, Sandy, a tongue like that would come in handy for stealing French fries from your friends at lunch. Think of the money you'd save.

Woodpeckers may not get headaches, but they sure can cause a few. Not a day goes by that I don't have to listen to someone complain about a woodpecker banging on his or her house. So, it was a nice change to get your question of concern about woodpeckers and possible headaches. Wait a minute, Sandy! Was this a question of concern or did I just do your seventh grade science project for you? If it is for your science project and *we* get an A, I want to know about it. It would be my first A and, boy, will my parents be proud.

## Wash-and-Wear Feathers

*Dear Bird Folks:*
*Last January when everything was frozen solid, flocks of star-*
*lings would come and splash about in my heated birdbath. When*
*my little cockatiel, Chip, takes a bath, she appears to get soaked*
*down to her pink skin. Why, when the temperature was so awful-*
*ly cold, wouldn't the starlings' water-soaked wings freeze solid?*
*Do starlings have some kind of Brylcreem gland that keeps the*
*water off their feathers?*

—*Anna,* SOMERVILLE, MA

What kind of gland, Anna?

Brylcreem? How old are you? I asked all my customers if they
knew what Brylcreem was and none of them did. Then one real
old guy spoke up and said, "I know what it is." Even after he told
us, we were still confused, but he is such a nice man we didn't
question him. I don't know his real name but his friends all call
him Fonzie. Perhaps you know him.

When you think about it, birds' feathers are truly a remarkable
invention. Feathers give most birds the ability to fly, which puts
birds in a league of their own (if you don't count bats and mos-
quitoes). Feathers also give each bird species its individuality.
Feathers create those amazing patterns that help distinguish a
Painted Bunting from a sparrow . . . or in your case, European
Starlings from Chip, the pink-skinned cockatiel. Without their
feathers, birds would be totally naked and unrecognizable, looking like something packaged by the late Frank Perdue.

Most importantly, feathers insulate birds from just about any
hostile environment. From the deep, dark frigid reaches of
Antarctica to the blasting heat of Africa, it is those tiny, seeming-

ly weightless feathers that enable birds to survive and thrive. And as you might expect, each species has its own unique set of feathers. Although neither of them can fly, it is fairly obvious that penguin feathers are quite different from those of an ostrich.

One thing that feathers excel at is shedding water. The expression "like water off a duck's back" applies to just about all birds, not just ducks and Fonzie's hair. Each single feather is made up of, for want of less confusing terms, many miniature feathers, which are linked together by tiny barbs. The barbs hold all the parts of the feather together so tightly that water can't penetrate. The next time you find a feather on the ground, hold it under a running faucet . . . for as long as you want. The feather, amazingly, will remain dry.

In addition to structural waterproofing, most birds' feathers are aided by an oil gland (a.k.a. the Brylcreem gland). The oil may help with waterproofing but more importantly, it keeps the feathers flexible. Brittle feathers don't hold up to the extremes that birds put them through.

After getting your note, Anna, I decided to test these theories. On one of those wicked cold days in January, when even the thermometers were frozen, I filled a small pool with water and released a family of pet ducks. Upon seeing the pool, the ducks raced across the yard, dove into the pool, and splashed and quacked like they had won the lottery. When all the craziness finally subsided, I picked up one of the ducks for an on-the-spot inspection. I found its feathers at every layer to be dry and ice-free. Only the very tips of the outer feathers had a few droplets of ice on them, which the duck immediately preened off.

European Starlings are one of the hardiest and most adaptable birds anywhere. Found on every continent, they don't seem to be affected by either extreme cold or heat. Cockatiels, with no offense to Chip and her relatives, are far more specialized. There is a reason why flocks of them aren't seen in cold climates; their pretty little feathers aren't designed for extreme snow and cold.

Each species has evolved to meet its geographic needs. Some birds are perfect for arid regions; others are totally at home on an ice floe, while still others seem to be equipped for many climates. As cute as Chip may be, she was not designed for dealing with and bathing in frigid weather. Not unless you first give her a Brylcreem comb-over. Perhaps you still have a tube of it in the glove box of your DeSoto.

## Flight Speed . . . and More

*Dear Bird Folks:*
*I often observe the birds in my yard flying across the pond. It appears they would do very well in a quarter-mile drag race. How fast do birds fly?*

—*Paul,* BREWSTER, MA

Great, Paul,

You had to mention drag racing. I knew it was only a matter of time before that surging NASCAR lingo worked its way to New England. Soon customers will be asking for bird feeders with STP or Goodyear stickers on them. They'll want to know if we sell binoculars with spoilers, and birders will begin taking birding trips to Daytona instead of the Everglades. It's only a matter of time.

Flying is what makes a bird a bird. (That last sentence is pretty profound so you may want to stop and write it down.) Mammals, the self-proclaimed premier creatures on the planet, have yet to master the art of flying (except for the lowly bat) unless they are willing to purchase a ticket two weeks in advance and wait in long lines. Flying is the mode most birds use to escape danger, search for food, attract a mate, and transport themselves from one backyard to the next or from one continent to another. Birds come in all shapes, sizes, and flying abilities. Some birds, such as quail, are only adequate flyers. They are more comfortable on the ground and only fly in short bursts when they are forced to. Hummingbirds, on the other hand, are astonishing flyers. They can hover, fly backward, or vanish instantly at the first sign of danger. With their lightning-quick speed, you would swear that hummers are the fastest of all birds. However, a hummingbird's speed is an illusion because of its size. They probably aren't even fast enough to keep up with those fat, old Canada geese.

Beside their physical abilities, other factors influence a bird's flight speed. Wind is a major factor. A flock of lapwings was reported to have made the 2,200-mile trip across the Atlantic, from Britain to Newfoundland, in a twenty-four-hour period. That's an average of ninety miles an hour. How was it possible for a flock of birds to fly at ninety miles per hour for twenty-four hours straight, and not get a ticket? They had the aid of a tailwind, which pushes birds much faster than they could ever flap on their own.

Most birds have several levels of speed. They fly fastest when they are pursuing prey or when they are being pursued as prey. Then there is the steady but urgent migration flight. A less hurried flight is used for short distances, like the birds flying across your pond. Finally there is the mega-slow speed that is found in birds that fly so slowly that all the other birds are backed up behind them. These birds usually only fly on Sunday and have Florida license plates.

With all of those factors in mind, it's pretty tough to accurately answer how fast birds fly. A good rule of thumb for most feeder birds is twenty miles per hour, but that can increase dramatically if there is trouble or if they need to catch a cab.

Remember, we are only talking feeder birds here. Other species of birds have been known to reach some ridiculous speeds. Years ago, the director of the local Audubon Society told me about seeing a merganser that was trapped in a small pool of water by a Bald Eagle. Every time the eagle attacked, the merganser would dive underwater. Slowly tiring from the attacks, the merganser decided to make a "run" for it and took off from the protection of the pool. Birders who were watching gasped, believing the duck had made a fatal mistake, only to be shocked as the merganser blew past the eagle like it was a stump. It turns out Red-breasted Mergansers are one of the fastest-flying ducks. One report claimed a merganser's escape speed can reach eighty miles per hour. Evidently, the hungry eagle never read that report and it had to settle for Chinese takeout that night.

The disputed title of the world's fastest bird is most often given to the Peregrine Falcon, which can reach speeds of over two hundred miles per hour. The title is disputed because the falcon only can reach those extreme speeds in a steep dive and not in level flight. Critics argue that the bird shouldn't be given credit since gravity is doing most of the work. Claims have also been made that in addition to gravity, the falcon gains extra power by using a HEMI, but you only hear that from the NASCAR crowd.

## Beak Talk

*Dear Bird Folks:*

*For you with your big mouth, this is not a problem. But how do birds like goldfinches, chickadees, and sparrows crack open those jumbo sunflower seeds with their teensy little beaks?*

—*John,* BREWSTER, MA

Brewster again, John? For some reason the vast majority of questions have come from Brewster lately. It seems as though everyone in Brewster is either very inquisitive or they all missed Bird Week in elementary school. Whatever. I'm happy to help and to . . . Wait a minute. Did you just call me a "bigmouth"? Listen here, Bucko, that's pretty brave talk from someone who apparently missed all of Bird Week. Don't worry. I don't really mind. I've been in a good mood since *Cats* closed on Broadway.

A while back, I emphatically stated that wings were the feature that made birds stand out above all creatures. Well, I was going through a dramatic phase. I've calmed down and have reconsidered. While it's true that wings are important, lots of creatures have wings. The beak is really the one thing that is unique to birds. Think about it. You really can't name one other creature on the entire planet that has a protruding beak . . . if you don't count Barbra Streisand.

(Just a quick side note: The terms "beak" and "bill" are interchangeable. Beaks and bills are one and the same. There, that should save me from having to answer a hundred more questions from Brewster.)

There is no doubt that the ability to fly is a huge advantage for birds, but having wings instead of arms and hands can lead to problems. Without hands, birds struggle to climb, dig, gather food, and juggle. Amazingly, birds' bills have adapted to take the place of hands or paws. With their beaks they can catch food, dig holes, build a nest, preen, care for their young, and defend themselves. Try any of those with your beak, John, and report back to me.

The birds' bills are extremely varied in both shape and size. Each species has developed a bill that can exploit a particular food source. Warblers have tiny beaks that they use to pluck minute insects off tree branches. Woodpeckers don't pluck but use their chisel bills to dig out insects buried deep inside trees or under the shingles of our houses. Many ducks have flat bills that they use to strain food out of pond water or mud. Shorebirds use their long bills to probe deep into the sand, while herons use their longer bills to spear fish. The obvious winner in the bill diversity race is the Roseate Spoonbill. Its odd spoon-shaped bill makes it one of the few birds that can eat soup without making a mess.

Finches and sparrows are seedeaters. They have cone-shaped beaks that are extremely strong and powerful. Bird banders will tell you that even the sissy cardinal can draw blood if not handled properly. A grosbeak lives up to its name by having the ability to open seeds that are as hard as cherry pits. Besides having strong and powerful beaks, most seedeaters also have sharp edges or grooves in their bills. It's these sharp edges that help the birds split open the tough seeds or the bird bander's hand.

Birds such as chickadees and nuthatches don't have those crushing finch beaks. They must hammer the seeds open. Chickadees hold the seed in their feet and hack away. Nuthatches, whose weird feet look more like skis, aren't able to hold seed and must jam it into a crevasse of a tree and "hatch" it open with their pointy bills. Even the beak of the muscle-bound Blue Jay isn't shaped correctly for snapping open seeds. They have their own way of feeding. Not wanting to look wimpy in front of other birds, a jay will swallow many seeds whole, fly someplace private, spit the seeds back up, and hammer them open like chickadees do.

Believe or not, John, I'm not the only bigmouth. Many birds have such tiny beaks that they must rely on their extra-large mouths to obtain food. Whip-poor-wills and nighthawks fly around in the dark with their massive mouths wide open, scooping up whatever insects get in their way. Like me, these birds have made a good living at being a bigmouth, although I don't enjoy sucking up the insects as much as they do.

## Hummingbird Beaks: Open Sesame

*Dear Bird Folks:*

*I know you receive tons of letters, but please answer this one for me. I have bet my great-aunt a box of Cuban cigars on this question. Do hummingbirds have beaks that open and close like other birds or do they sip through a one-piece, strawlike beak that doesn't open?*

*—Rowdy,* ORLEANS, MA

First of all, Rowdy,

If you are going to ask a question like this, don't use your real nickname. Try to be a little more ambiguous. How many Rowdys can there be in Orleans now that summer is over? You could be setting yourself up for ridicule. As you walk down the street, all of your friends will be pointing at you and chanting, "Rowdy, Rowdy, what a freak, doesn't know much about hummingbird beaks." Then there is the issue of tipping off the U.S. Customs Department about your Cuban cigar racket. I'm sure they read this stuff faithfully. Finally, betting is illegal. I'll lay you ten to one that the Massachusetts State Gaming Commission will be interested in your little gambling ring.

As for your hummingbird question, do you or your great-aunt really believe a hummingbird's beak is some kind of one-piece sucking straw? I think someone is smoking more than cigars. Or perhaps one of you has hummingbirds mixed up with an elephant and its trunk. I can see how you would get those two confused. Hummingbirds are birds, real birds, and they have everything that a robin or cardinal has, including feet, legs, wings, and a beak that acts and works like any other bird's beak.

Much of a hummingbird's diet is composed of insects. They obtain these insects by using their superior flying skills, along with their beak and tongue, to snag insects out of the air, not by sucking bugs out of the sky. Perhaps you are thinking of the Hoover Flycatcher. That species is excellent at sucking up insects, not to mention dust bunnies.

As for nipping nectar from flowers, their beak has little to do with it. It is the hummingbird's extremely long tongue that does most of the work. A hummingbird's tongue is split at the end, with tiny hairlike fibers that help gather nectar from flowers. The tongue features extra folds that are a bit brushy, which makes it easier to lap up nectar. A hummingbird's tongue can lap at the rate of thirteen times per second, just like my neighbor's golden retriever.

Even though a hummingbird's beak isn't the key feature in gathering nectar, the beak is essential for grooming and preening. Feathers are the birds' only protection from the elements and it is critical that they keep them neat and clean. Hummingbirds use their long beaks to regularly groom their feathers. They use the beak to grasp each feather and clean off dirt and parasites, while also adding protective oil to their feathers.

And let's not forget those nest-building chores, Rowdy. The hummer's beak is the only tool it has to build its nest. The female gathers the material and constructs the nest using nothing more than her beak. If her beak weren't able to open, there would be no way for the mother to feed the baby birds. The adult bird shoves insects down the wide-open gape of the hungry baby. With your tube beak idea, feeding the babies would be rather difficult, not to mention messy. A tube-to-tube connection would be impossible without a plumber, and who can get one of those to show up, especially at dinnertime?

I don't know who is going to win the bet, Rowdy, but the answer to your question is: Hummingbirds most assuredly can open and close their beaks. Betting a box of Cuban cigars over a bird question may sound a little strange, but who am I to judge? I think it's cool that you have such a fun relationship with your great-aunt. The only thing I ever bet my great-aunt was that she couldn't eat a caramel apple with her false teeth. I won the bet, but I had to buy her a new set of teeth. That could have been expensive but fortunately I got lucky at the local swap shed.

## Snoozing Birds

*Dear Bird Folks:*
*Once again I turn to the bird guru for a profound answer to this serious question. How and where do birds sleep? Do you have any pictures of them sleeping?*

—*Dick,* CHATHAM, MA

Say what, Dick?

A guru? You think I'm a guru? Wait until the kids from the old neighborhood find out about this. We used to sit around talking about who would be the first one to become a guru. I was never high on the list . . . guess I showed them.

Sleep is quite different for birds than it is for us. Birds don't have the eight-hour, dead-to-the-world snore fest like we do. They are totally light sleepers, rarely falling into any kind of deep sleep. Most of us are able to sleep soundly without much fear of being eaten. But birds must be constantly aware of their surroundings, keeping an ear alert for danger, ready to hop out of "bed" and move on at a moment's notice. Short bursts of sleep are the best that many of them can hope for.

Where do birds sleep? Birds typically roost in the same type of habitat they nest in. Ducks sleep in or near water; shorebirds sleep on the beach; cardinals sleep in bushes; woodpeckers sleep in, of all places, woodpecker holes. I'm not sure what bird you had in mind when you asked this question, Dick, but whatever bird it was, think about where it lives and that is where it probably roosts. City pigeons eat and sleep in the middle of town; they don't fly to the beach to sleep. And sandpipers at the beach don't fly to the roof of town hall to spend the night. The one exception is the plastic flamingo, which leaves the wetlands to spend the night in a trailer park.

As for how they sleep, most birds use the old "wing tuck" method. Birds don't actually tuck their heads under their wing. Instead, they rest their heads on their backs while they nuzzle their beaks into their back feathers. Sleeping that way allows birds to rest their neck muscles and also makes for better heat conservation.

Quail, such as Bobwhites, huddle together on the ground in a tight circle with their heads facing out, ready for a quick getaway. Sea ducks sleep while bobbing around in the open ocean. And most shorebirds spend the night on outer beaches with their heads tucked on their backs, while they sleep standing on one leg. (Don't ask about the one-leg thing, Dick. Let's save that question for someone else.)

Like most things in the bird world, there are a few freak birds that do something totally off the wall. Some parrots cling to branches upside down, sleeping like bats. Some swifts never land, except to breed. Most of the year swifts continue to fly nonstop, day and night. It is commonly thought that swifts sleep on the wing. And giraffes sleep less than thirty minutes a day. I know that last fact has nothing to do with birds, but where else can I use that odd piece of information?

Thanks for the question, Dick, and thanks for thinking I'm a guru. However, I can't supply you with any pictures of birds sleeping. You'll probably have to go to some weird adult website to find those kinds of pictures.

## One-Legged Birds with No Ears . . . No Problem

*Dear Bird Folks:*
*Why do birds sleep standing on one leg? My aunt has a pigeon and we were wondering about this behavior. Also, how are they able to hear so well without the benefit of large ears, like mammals have? I hope I'm not cheating by asking two questions at once but I would really appreciate the answers to both.*
—*Emily,* TUPPER LAKE, NY

It's okay, Emily,

I don't mind two questions. Wondering about birds' hearing is an excellent question. It is odd that birds can hear so well without appearing to have ears. As for the standing-on-one-leg thing, I knew it was only a matter of time before that question came up. I might as well answer it now and get it over with.

Birds do indeed have excellent hearing but like most things in nature, there are different designs for different creatures. Most land mammals have significant outer ears, or pinnas (look it up; it's a real word). Pinna size is not as important as many people think. If having large external ears allowed mammals to hear more, Ross Perot would be listening to us right now. And elephants would have the best hearing of all when, in fact, elephants' hearing is relatively poor. Their huge external ears are mostly used for cooling, defense posturing, and in the case of Dumbo, flying.

Bird hearing is at best complicated and at worst boring to read about. I'm afraid if I get into too many details even people in prison will put down this book and go back to staring at the walls. You should know, however, that it is the internal ear that is the key to birds' hearing. The ear openings of birds are larger than you might think; it's just that they are covered with feathers. In many cases, the feathers are arranged to help channel sounds into the bird's ear.

For years, keen-eared birds have been used as "watchdogs," or in this case, "watchbirds." Before the days of radar, trained parrots were used in the military. The parrots could hear the hum of distant enemy planes and would squawk a warning long before the planes could be heard by humans. Pigeons also have excellent hearing. (So, your aunt had better be careful what she says about hers.) In addition to visual cues, homing pigeons apparently use audio clues (ocean sounds, waterfalls, etc.) to find their way back to the roost.

Now, for your second question. Man, I would love to have a doughnut for every time someone came screaming to me about seeing a bird with a leg missing. Tucking up one leg is very common for birds to do, yet no one knows for sure why. The most prevalent theory is that it's to conserve heat. As you know, most birds have bare naked legs, without the covering of insulating feathers; by tucking up one leg, a bird can at least have that leg insulated from the cold. Go to any beach parking lot in the winter and you'll see dozens of one-legged gulls looking like they are ready to tip over.

That insulation idea makes sense, until you think about flamingos living in the zillion-degree heat of Florida. Why would they need to keep warm? The thought here is that they lift one foot simply to give it a chance to dry out. Standing in wet mud 24/7 has to be tough on a new pedicure. Another theory is that by standing on one leg, flamingos change their silhouette and thus are able to fool predators into thinking they are some kind of odd vegetation. Although I think the real problem in trying to hide is not the number of legs, but the bright, fluorescent pink feathers. But what do I know?

Why would your aunt's pigeon, living in a warm, cozy house, sleep on one leg? It probably stems from its wild heritage. Either that or your aunt's house has some serious draft issues.

## Sorry, Robins Aren't the First Bird of Spring

*Dear Bird Folks:*
*All my life I have happily believed that the robin is the first bird of spring. It gave me great comfort knowing that when the robins arrived, spring was on the way. Well, all that comfort ended when I read one of your recent columns. You coldly stated that robins are with us year round and thus cannot be used as indicators of nicer weather. Fine, I can accept that. But if the robin is no longer the first bird, which bird is? And when will it finally get here? I've had enough of this nasty winter.*

*—Artie,* ALLENTOWN, PA

Sorry, Artie,
I'm sorry for spoiling your warm, fuzzy story about the robins. Even though it may be true that robins aren't the first sign of

spring, that's no reason to think any less of them. Heck, without the robin we would be in danger of being overrun by worms. Earthworms have developed a sophisticated and dangerous underground movement. It's the robins that stand between us and total worldwide worm domination. At least that's what I read at the supermarket checkout line.

The first bird of spring really depends upon where you live. For parts of northern New England and most of Canada, the American Robin may very well be the first migrant of spring. It is absent from those areas during the winter. In my neighborhood, we see robins every day of the year so their appearance doesn't mean better weather is coming. The bird that means spring to me is a Thunderbird, a candy-apple red Thunderbird convertible, driven by Lloyd Townsend, a guy who lives around the corner. Ol' Lloyd's car stays wrapped up in his heated garage, hibernating until winter passes. When I see that red T-bird cruising down the road, I know that spring is here for sure.

You are right to look for birds as a sign of spring, Artie, because birds are amazingly reliable indicators. Insects and plants can be fooled by a warm spell. We've all seen flies buzzing around on an unseasonably warm day in January. A warm winter's day will also convince crocus bulbs to start sprouting, only to be buried under snow and ice for another eight weeks. Birds, however, aren't fooled by the occasional warm spell.

Why aren't birds fooled? How are they able to accurately know when it's time to migrate? Since few birds can afford watches and even fewer can figure out how to adjust them for daylight savings time, they have another way of determining time. Birds have photoreceptors at the base of their brains that record the length of day. Oddly, the birds don't measure the amount of daylight, but they apparently focus on the amount of darkness (talk about being negative). Then they somehow are able to do the math and conclude that shorter nights equal longer days and longer days mean spring is on the way.

My favorite returning bird of spring, besides Lloyd's T-bird, is the American Woodcock. Woodcocks are prehistoric-looking, long-beaked woodland "shorebirds," which resemble water balloons with handles. They appear to be far too fragile and goofy to survive a night of fog, let alone a late winter snowstorm. But by the end of every February, reports come streaming in from people who have been hearing returning woodcocks perform their mating ritual.

A far more common signal that spring is returning is the reappearance of Red-winged Blackbirds. Amazingly, as soon as late February or early March, redwings are back, ready to begin the breeding season again. Some locations have redwings year round, but only when winter is winding down do we hear the males as they settle back into the marshes and sing their signature *konk-le-reee* song.

And let's not forget our backyard goldfinches. Even though goldfinches visit many of our yards every day of the year, a sure sign of spring is when, in early March, the males start shedding their winter coats and we see flecks of gold showing through their dull green winter plumage.

You know, Artie, you can still use your beloved robins as a sign of spring, but not those robins that you see in large flocks eating fruit from bushes. It's the robins we see running across our lawns, protecting us from the next earthworm attack, that tell us winter is on the way out.

By carefully studying the ways of nature, you will begin to appreciate the subtle clues that can tip you off as to which season is coming and which season is going. Either that or go out and buy yourself a calendar, which isn't a bad idea since they are on sale right now.

## To Touch or Not to Touch Baby Birds

*Dear Bird Folks:*
*Once in a while my kids find baby birds that have fallen out of*
*their nests. The kids want to take them home and feed them. I've*
*always thought that we should just leave them alone. What's the*
*best thing to do?*

—*Ethel,* WORCESTER, MA

You know, Ethel,

All my life I have been accused of taking the easy way out. If I
spilled food, it was easier to let the dog lap it up than actually use
a mop. If I lost the remote control, it was easier to keep watching
*Meet the Press* than to get up and look for the remote so I could
change the channel. So, when I read that you'd rather leave the
baby bird alone instead of taking it home to care for it, by my
nature I have to agree with you. However, in this case, doing nothing is probably the best thing to do. Being lazy sometimes works
if you give it a chance.

Many baby birds leave the nest before they can fly and spend
a day or two on the ground while the parents continue to feed
them. Instead of scooping up the bird, just watch it for a few
hours and I think you'll find that the parents are still around.

Really young birds that have few feathers need to be picked up
and returned to the nest. Before you start screaming about the
mother bird detecting your scent and abandoning the baby, keep
in mind that songbirds aren't in the habit of sniffing their
nestlings. In fact, it's questionable how good their sense of smell
really is. If a songbird is able to detect your smell, you may want
to lay off the garlic.

If you can't find the nest, make one out of a small basket and
place it in the closest tree. Again, you need to step back and watch

to see if the parents return to care for the baby bird. In all cases, if after two hours you see no signs of the parent birds, then you should take the next step. Capture the baby bird, keep it quiet in a darkened box (without food, water, or magazines), and call the nearest wildlife rehabilitator. (You usually can find one in the phone book or online.)

The important thing to remember is that the baby bird's parents will do the best job of caring for it. Unless there are other dangers around like kids, dogs, or the "C"-word (cats), just wait and watch for the parent birds to do their job. You could also try filling your mouth with worms and feeding the bird yourself, but I suspect it's easier to call a wildlife rehabilitator.

## Where Babies Come From

*Dear Bird Folks:*
*I am new around here, very new. The only bird that I know about is the stork. I would very much like to know why the stork was chosen to deliver babies to their families.*
*—Hannah J., ten days old,* NORTH EASTHAM, MA

Welcome, Hannah J.,

It is always nice to have a new reader. You have very good writing skills for being only ten days old. I couldn't write that well until I was almost fifteen days old.

Like most traditions in this country, the stork thing started in a wacky part of the world called Europe. Storks winter in Africa but return to Europe every spring to nest on the roofs of farmhouses. Spring is a time of birth in Europe; new cows are born as well as horses, goats, and the occasional troll. The coming of spring is important because most farm couples hope to have their children arrive in the spring so they'll be big enough to help in the fields come summer.

Storks are strong and powerful fliers and can easily carry even the biggest baby to the farmer. Other birds that return to the farms in the spring, such as swallows, are only able to deliver very small children. And small children are not well suited for farm work. The long beak is also an advantage. Storks are able to pick up the baby by hooking the diaper on their beaks. That is very important because for hundreds of years the EPA has required all babies wear diapers while being flown over crowded neighborhoods.

Storks eat frogs, mice, snakes, and even young birds. So, new babies are being delivered by flying carnivores, which is an interesting thought. But it should be noted that there is no record of a stork ever eating a baby. Although there are perhaps a few they should have eaten.

Other countries have tried different methods of delivering babies, but the stork has beaten them out every time. Australia used to have kangaroos deliver the babies, since the pouch is such a comfortable way to travel. However, all the jumping caused way too much motion sickness. Most babies don't need another excuse to spit up, so the kangaroo method was abandoned.

In this country, we tried pelicans for a while. Pelicans seemed like a perfect fit. The babies could ride in the pelican's big, roomy bottom beak and they didn't even need to wear a diaper. And if it began to rain, the kids could simply shut the top beak and stay dry. However, many parents complained about the fish smell on their new children. And since babies have enough odd smells, the pelican idea was eventually dropped. Even UPS gave baby delivering a shot, but they had a problem with the shipping labels not sticking to the new babies' soft and slippery skin. A few label-less babies were lost in shipping (and somehow ended up at my house).

So there you go, Hannah J. I hope that answers your question. My research found many more examples of baby delivery methods over the years but the stork has always won out. And judging by the large number of school buses I'm always getting stuck behind, they are doing a great job.

## Rice Is Nice . . . and Safe, Too

*Dear Bird Folks:*
*I'm the maid of honor at my sister's spring wedding. Before I do too much planning I need to know if it is really okay to throw rice. Some people tell me rice is bad for birds and that we should throw birdseed instead. You are probably going to tell me to throw birdseed since that is what you sell, but is rice really that bad?*
*—Kathy, EASTHAM, MA*

Hold on, Kathy,
Are you saying I would purposely mislead you in order to sell more birdseed? Well, I am ashamed. I'm not ashamed of you, but of myself for not thinking about doing that before. What a great idea. If the economy doesn't improve soon, I just might answer

every question with "Buy birdseed," no matter what the question is. But right now you'll have to settle for the truth. Or at least the truth the way I see it.

Here's the theory on wedding rice. As the happy couple leaves the church, all their so-called friends show their love by pelting them with fistfuls of hard, uncooked rice. If they somehow are able to survive that, the couple drives away and the tossed rice is left lying unguarded on the sidewalk. Soon a flock of innocent birds arrives to chow down whatever rice didn't get lodged in the target victims' eyes, ears, and underwear. Once ingested, the harmless rice quickly expands to 50,000 times its original size, causing the birds to inflate to roughly the size of the *Hindenburg*. Not only is this rapid expansion bad for the birds, but the birds' massive bodies can block traffic for hours.

This might come as a surprise to many, but rice is a grain. Grains, seeds, and nuts are what birds have survived on for centuries. Ask any rice farmer and they will tell you that they can only hope that birds will overinflate upon stealing their rice. The rice that thousands of birds are eating in rice fields every day is the same rice you buy in the store and throw at weddings. Rice, cooked or uncooked, will not bother the birds. But I wouldn't throw cooked rice at your sister's wedding without checking with her first or without letting it cool.

There is nothing wrong with throwing rice at weddings or whenever you are in the mood to throw stuff at people. But good or bad, if I were you, Kathy, I still would throw birdseed. Birdseed is trendy. Plus, the local birds will enjoy it more than rice. And if you bought a whole pound of seed from me, I would finally pass Bill Gates on the *Forbes* richest man in the world list. Won't he be surprised?

While I'm on the subject of myths, here's another one. Rumor has it if you toss a gull an Alka-Seltzer, the gull will eat it and explode. That's right, explode. Listen, Alka-Seltzer might taste bad but it's not dynamite; it's medicine. Do you really think they would sell it to people if it made things explode? All it does is produce gas, and most creatures have a way ridding themselves of gas with only small explosions. Like many birds, gulls are masters at regurgitating things that don't agree with them. Even though they may not explode, I'm certainly not recommending anyone give gulls Alka-Seltzer. Although, after what I've seen gulls eat, they probably wouldn't mind a few tablets.

## Heroic State Bird of Utah

*Dear Bird Folks:*
*A poster in our school says that the state bird of Utah is the seagull. Isn't Utah a long way from the sea? Why would they choose a seagull as their state bird?*

*—Jason, Grade 8,* PLYMOUTH, MA

Hey, Jason,

If you think the gull thing is nuts, listen to these other birds that have been chosen as state birds. Our neighbor, Rhode Island, has the chicken as its state bird. That's right, they chose an honest-to-goodness chicken. Who was governor then? Frank Perdue? And some bonehead in South Dakota picked the Ring-necked Pheasant as its state bird. That's a good one. Pheasants aren't even from this continent. Come on. Of the hundreds of different bird species that are native to South Dakota, they couldn't find one they liked? North Dakota didn't have any trouble. They chose the Western Meadowlark, a wonderful bird.

A pheasant? (Honest, Jason, I'll get to your question in a minute. Just let me finish my rant.) Pheasants are from Asia. They are an introduced species, in the same category as Japanese beetles, the Hong Kong flu, and Robin Leach.

Then there is the cardinal (I'm almost done). At last count, something like seventy-five states have picked the cardinal as the state bird. Hello? We have over seven hundred bird species in this country. Is it too hard to choose a bird that hasn't been taken by a ton of other states already? That's it. I'm done.

After all that, you may be surprised to learn that I think the seagull is an excellent choice for Utah. Here is why. Back in 1848, the crops of the early Mormon settlers were being wiped out. A massive plague of cricket-locust things were chowing down all their crops. The poor Mormons didn't know what to do, except to pray, of course. One guy tried leading them away by playing the flute, but he only ended up attracting rats. That worked out okay because the rats were instantly eaten by the locusts.

Suddenly, just when the Mormons thought their crops were about to be totaled, a massive flock of seagulls appeared out of nowhere. The seagulls wolfed down every bug in town, saved the crops, and prevented the Mormons from having to go out to dinner for the entire winter.

This story is definitely true, but I have one problem. It's the name "seagull." The name "seagull" is a generic name wrongly given to gulls. "Gull" is generic enough; the "sea" part should not be added because the sea is not important to many gulls. Millions of gulls live far inland and never get near the ocean, except with their families for two weeks in the summer. Gulls do like to be near water, but it doesn't need to be saltwater. Any large lake or even a river will do fine.

The gulls that saved the settlers were California Gulls, but they didn't fly in from California just to help the Mormons. California Gulls live in Utah year-round. What the Mormons thought was a miracle (so the story goes) was simply a flock of California Gulls that nested at the nearby Great Salt Lake, eating the same crickets they have been eating for many years. California Gulls look much like the Herring Gulls that we see around the Northeast, only California Gulls are a bit smaller. Their smaller size is probably due to some crazy West Coast diet that has become popular in recent years.

If you ever get to Salt Lake City, Jason, you can see a huge statue erected to the California Gull. Unfortunately, the statue says "Sea Gull" on it, not California Gull. However, it is still better than having a huge statue of a Ring-necked Pheasant or Robin Leach.

## The Birder's Bird Watcher

*Dear Bird Folks:*

*I read your recent column on the Great Auk with great enjoyment. But you wrote that the Great Auk was "North America's only flightless bird." If Guatemala is in North America, and I believe it is, you should consider the flightless Lake Atitlan Grebe, which is also now extinct. I mention this because the bird was discovered and was given its Latin name by my father, ornithologist Ludlow Griscom.*

*—Andrew Griscom, CHATHAM, MA*

You know, Andrew,

Your note started out so good, then I saw the dreaded "but" and I knew I was a dead man. The "buts" always mean trouble ahead. I should have stopped reading right after the words "great enjoyment." That's what I get for being nosy.

Of course, you are right about Guatemala being in North America. For anyone who might be running to the nearest atlas thinking that Guatemala is in Central America and not North America, forget it. I tried that. Central America is indeed considered part of North America.

Not wanting to drag everyone down with another extinction story, I've decided not to dwell on the loss of that little grebe. I'd rather write something a bit more positive. With due respect, Andrew, I would like to pass along a few words to the readers about your father, for it would be hard to find anyone who has had a more positive effect on the world of birding than Ludlow Griscom.

If you were to ask the average person to identify the biggest names in bird watching, they would probably say John James Audubon, me, Roger Tory Peterson, and in recent times, David Allen Sibley. Besides me, those other three guys have one thing that distinguishes them from Ludlow Griscom. Can you guess what it is? They all have middle names. Wasn't it obvious? The other important difference is that those three icons were talented artists. Their works and their names were out there for the masses to learn and recognize. Griscom, on the other hand, was a birdman. He didn't spend endless hours in the studio and on book tours; he spent them in the field, educating other birders and promoting the protection of important habitat.

It was Ludlow Griscom who first taught the young Roger Tory Peterson the skills of field identification. Before Griscom, there really were no "birders." Anyone interested in birds was either a collector or an ornithologist, and both studied birds up close via the "shotgun method." Using the skills he learned from Griscom and his artistic talents, Peterson produced a revolutionary field guide to birds. Back in the 1930s, Peterson's field guide concept was so unusual that publisher after publisher refused to print it. It was the Boston-based Houghton Mifflin Company that finally took a chance and printed a mere 2,000 copies . . . but not until they showed the book to Ludlow Griscom for his approval. That book passed the Griscom test and went on to sell close to a zillion copies.

Ludlow Griscom is not a name from the distant past like Audubon, or from another country like Darwin. Griscom spent most of his adult life in Massachusetts, working at Harvard

University's Museum of Comparative Zoology. Spending summers in his house in Chatham, Massachusetts, Griscom led legendary birding trips to Monomoy (a barrier beach that extends south off the "elbow" of the Cape, and is a critical nesting and staging area for migrating shorebirds).

Many longtime Cape birders have told me stories of those trips. They would float an old car across to Monomoy and drive along the beach in search of birds. The car itself was half the show. We are not talking about a luxury SUV with AC, a DVD player, and GPS. Griscom drove a wooden-paneled Model A Ford with balloon tires that got stuck much of the time.

Griscom's lifetime of achievements is more than impressive. He was president of the American Ornithologist Union. Okay, fine; that doesn't mean much to me either, but he was also chairman of the board of the National Audubon Society. Even Audubon himself never did that. Griscom was a driving force in the Massachusetts Audubon Society and is given credit for putting Boston's Museum of Science on the map and saving it from bankruptcy. It was through his efforts that both Parker River on Plum Island in Newburyport, MA, and Monomoy became National Wildlife Refuges. And don't let me forget to mention that somehow Ludlow Griscom found time to travel to the tropics, where he discovered several new bird species including the now famous flightless Lake Atitlan Grebe.

While others in the birding world, because of their skills and successful publications, have reached celebrity status, Ludlow Griscom achieved legendary status in the eyes of his peers. Sometimes that's all the notoriety anyone ever needs.

## Backyard Birds Aren't Meant to Be Worn

*Dear Bird Folks:*

*I recently came upon a book with the horrifying title* She's Wearing a Dead Bird on Her Head. *The book turned out to be written for children and is about the formation of the Audubon Society. After I left the store, I started thinking about this odd book. Have you ever heard of this book and do you know if the story is fictitious or is it based on real events?*

—*Margie,* MUNCIE, IN

My little Margie,

I'm not about to give you a hard time for reading a book in the store instead of forking over the tremendous sum of $6.99 to buy it. I do the same thing. But if you had flipped to the ending, like I always do, you would have known that, yes, the book was indeed based on real events. Over one hundred years ago, fashionable women would wear hats that were so ridiculous looking that snowboarders would have been jealous. These so-called fashionable hats were made out of freshly killed backyard birds.

For hundreds of years people would wear a single plume in their hats. The feather-in-the-hat design can be traced to such fashion-conscious notables as the Pied Piper and Yankee Doodle. Although the birds weren't thrilled with this idea, the single plume was an arrangement they could live with. Then, somewhere around the end of the nineteenth century, it all went wrong. Rich women decided that if one feather was cool, wearing the entire bird would make them downright happenin'. So instead of a plume or two, sometimes the entire bird was sewn onto the hat: feet, beak, gizzards, and all.

Things were so bad that in 1886, a New York ornithologist stood on a Manhattan street corner and identified the birds that passed him on the sidewalk. The list included bluebirds, hummingbirds, orioles, warblers, and owls. On that one day he counted one hundred and seventy dead birds riding on the tops of one hundred and seventy hats, followed by one hundred and seventy hungry cats.

Ten years later, a Boston socialite named Harriet Hemenway decided enough was enough. She called her cousin Minna and together they organized a series of afternoon teas. (For the rest of you, Harriet and Minna are the stars of the aforementioned book that Margie was too cheap to buy.) During these teas, it was suggested to the other socialite women of Boston that birds could be better enjoyed sitting in trees than on the hats of the rich. The other ladies agreed and thus began the Massachusetts Audubon Society, the country's oldest Audubon Society.

Harriet and Minna were not the minimalist earthy tree huggers of today. They were part of Boston's respected upper crust. However, upper crust or not, they were still women and in 1896, women were anything but a powerful social force. They could not vote. Most weren't allowed to have meaningful jobs. And in many areas they weren't even allowed to drive cars, although much of that had to do with the fact that cars hadn't been invented yet.

These women may not have had much power, but their husbands were tremendously powerful; with their help, the word was spread that the fashion industry was needlessly destroying our native bird population. Within months, Audubon societies sprang up in other states, all voicing the same concerns. In 1900, four years after Harriet and Minna started their afternoon teas, the Lacy Act was passed. The Lacy Act, which banned the transportation of illegally killed birds across state lines, was the first of a string of victories for the preservation of birds. The most powerful of these victories was the Migratory Bird Act of 1913. That act clearly saved many familiar birds from extinction.

Stopping the slaughter of birds might seem like a no-brainer today, but in 1896 shootin' stuff was a way of life for many people. Killing birds for the millinery trade was a profitable business. The bird protection acts put thousands of people out of work. Not unlike the commercial fishing and logging battles of recent years, keeping birds off hats in 1896 was not as cut-and-dry as it sounds today. It was no easy task for the two non-voting, non-driving women from Boston.

With this one cause, Harriet and Minna were not only at the forefront of the conservation movement, they also made a statement for the fledgling women's movement. If turn-of-the-century women wanted to be taken seriously by their male counterparts, they could no longer walk around with a head full of hummingbirds.

Luckily for our birds, modern women don't feel compelled to make silly fashion statements as in years gone by. Today's females are quite content keeping things simple with low-waisted jeans, tattoos, and pierced tongues.

## How Bird Watching Can Improve Your Life

*Dear Bird Folks:*
*A recent edition of* U.S. News & World Report *had an extensive article entitled "50 Ways to Improve Your Life." One suggestion that surprised me was that we should take up bird watching. Granted it was way down at No. 46, but still, they included it. Do you really think that someone's life could be improved by bird watching?*

—*Deb,* EASTHAM, MA

Surprised, Deb?
You were surprised that bird watching made the list of the best

ways to improve your life and that it came in at No. 46? Are you kidding? Dude, it should have been No. 1. What could improve your life more than bird watching? Well, sure, you and I could both think of a few things that might be better than birding, but believe me they weren't on that list. After receiving your question I checked out the article. I am now more convinced than ever that bird watching should have been The Number One Way to Improve Your Life. Let's take a look at a few of the other recommendations, shall we?

Here's one: "Grow a plant." This suggestion came in at No. 12. Unless you are a farmer or a drug dealer, growing a plant isn't going to improve your life, especially if it's a houseplant. Houseplants have all the excitement of a bookmark, but with lots of maintenance. How many times have you had to ask, "Did you water the plants?" A plant just adds stress and worry. And when the plant dies, you are faced with the guilt. Stress, worry, and guilt—all because of a plant. And what do you get in return? A little oxygen, some dried leaves, and aphids. I say ditch the plant and keep the aphids . . . at least they move.

If you think growing a plant is dull, take a look at No. 3: "Clean your closet." Yes, you read that right, and it's No. 3. I don't want to put anybody down here, but your life is in pretty bad shape if sprucing up your closet is considered a major improvement.

Some of the other suggestions might have been good ones if they didn't conflict with each other. No. 10 is "Quit your job." Okay, fine. Getting out of a dead-end job should be an improvement, but that all changes with No. 17: "Fix your finances." I may be overthinking this, but wouldn't it be tough to fix your finances after you have just quit your job? It's not going to work unless No. 18 is "Rob a bank."

The list goes on and some ideas aren't bad. No. 2 is a good one: "Learn to meditate." I think that used to be called "taking a nap," but nevertheless, the occasional rest is important. However,

"Becoming a birder" is clearly the best thought on the entire list. Bird watching has it all. Let us count the ways.

A morning bird walk is a peaceful way to get some fresh air and exercise without getting sweaty. You can walk slowly, studying every bird as you go or you can walk at a faster pace and simply enjoy their early morning songs. And the best part is that bird walks don't have to be in the morning. If you are a late sleeper or just plain lazy, take an evening walk; the owls will enjoy the company.

No. 11 on the list is "Use your gray matter." Let me tell you something. Discovering cold fusion takes less brainpower than trying to identify sparrows or shorebirds. If you want to keep your brain sharp, spend a September afternoon on some mudflats trying to put names to the hundreds of scurrying generic shorebirds. Some species will be brown, some will be light brown, some will be gray-brown, some will be grayish-brown, some will be grayish-brownish, some will be lightish-grayish-lightish-brownish . . . and they all will be moving. Good luck.

Birding can be done at any level you choose. Nobody likes to ride with a bad driver, eat food prepared by a bad cook, or listen to a bad singer, but it doesn't matter with birding. Even if you stink at it, nobody minds. Most people I see every day actually know very little about birds, but they know they enjoy seeing them and for most of us, that's plenty.

Whose life has been improved by bird watching, Deb? I say anyone who tries it will notice an improvement. Whether you take it to the extremes of the hard-core birder, choose the relaxed style of the backyard bird watcher, or become a money-grubbing bird capitalist like myself, it is all good. And if for some reason birding doesn't improve your life, you can go for No. 3 and "clean your closet." But just be emotionally prepared for the excitement cleaning a closet will bring.

## Got to Have a Favorite Bird

*Dear Bird Folks:*
*At a party the other night we were discussing our favorite birds.*
*Then we started wondering what your favorite bird is. We all*
*took a guess and my job was to write to you to find out if any of*
*us was right. So, what is your favorite bird?*

— *Monica,* BARNSTABLE, MA

Really, Monica?

You went to a party and played "Name your favorite bird"?
Talk about living on the edge. Did the cops break it up? I hope
your kids don't find out what you people do at night.

My favorite bird, eh? I feel like I'm being interviewed for a
teen magazine. Fine, I'll tell you my favorite bird. Maybe next

week I'll tell you my favorite movie, my sign, and my turn-ons and turn-offs.

As far as I'm concerned, all birds are great. They all have fascinating behaviors, incredible survival skills, and diversified beauty. Yet, only one bird has all the best qualities wrapped up in one neat package. The Black-capped Chickadee is by far the best bird ever invented. I know, right now there are millions of readers (or at least dozens) screaming, "Chickadee? No way!" To which I reply, "Way." Chickadees have it all.

First, they are so stinkin' cute. Many birds have flashier colors, but with the fancy colors comes a snotty attitude. The beautiful spring warblers can't be bothered coming close enough for us to appreciate their colors. They zip about high in the treetops and couldn't care less that we suffer permanent neck damage staring straight up for hours, hoping for a glimpse. Meanwhile, the inquisitive little chickadee will come to the branch just above your head, or will even land on your head if you are pleasant enough and if your hair is clean.

For a guy who makes a living selling bird stuff, chickadees are the perfect bird. They eat just about every type of seed and they love suet. They nest in birdhouses and they come to birdbaths. Chickadees alone could put my kids through college if, for some reason, one of my kids was accepted at a college.

Over the course of a year, Cape Cod is visited by close to three hundred and fifty different species of birds, but very few can claim that they are here year round. Some birds (and many people) hate the heat, hate the cold, and/or hate the crowds. To them the grass is always greener. But our chickadees are with us 24/7/365. They are able to deal with the hot, crowded summers and have learned to adapt to the freezing, boring winters. And never once do they complain about either. How many of you can say that?

Speaking of complaining, have you ever heard anyone complain about a chickadee? Has its sweet song ever woken you up at 6 A.M. or have they ever taken a bite out of anything in your garden? Have they ever made a mess on your boat or drilled holes in the side of your house or charged anything on your credit card without permission? I'm telling you, these birds are perfect.

I know there are plenty of cardinal fans screaming that cardinals are the best. Please. Cardinals are a bunch of sissies. Think about it. Anytime there is a predator around, crows, jays, and chickadees are the first ones to sound the alarm. Meanwhile the cardinals are nowhere to be seen. Most of the time they don't even show up at our feeders until it's almost dark.

Keep in mind, Monica, that I enjoy all birds. Just because I think chickadees are the best (and they are) doesn't mean other birds aren't wonderful. Okay, maybe calling cardinals a bunch of sissies was a little harsh, but I'm not taking it back.

## Shorter Answers

*Dear Bird Folks:*
*I enjoy reading your column every week but sometimes the answers run a bit long. I have to read through many paragraphs before I find the real answer to the question. Any chance of writing shorter answers?*

—*Jeff,* CHATHAM, MA

Dear Jeff,
No.

**Mike O'Connor** is the owner of the Bird Watcher's General Store on Cape Cod. His column, Ask the Bird Folks, appears in *The Cape Codder,* and his writing has been included in *Good Birders Don't Wear White* and *The Best American Science and Nature Writing 2004.* He often goes birding in Cape Cod National Seashore's Beech Forest, in Provincetown, where the chickadees greet him when arrives. He would like us to think that the Beech Forest birds are drawn to him, and that's true. They are drawn to him . . . and to anyone else who offers them a hand filled with birdseed.*

*Note: The National Park Service discourages people from feeding birds on their property, so this has to be our little secret.